The Critical Hindu

H.V. BHATT

ॐ असतो मा सद्गमय ।
तमसो मा ज्योतिर्गमय ।
मृत्योर्मा अमृतं गमय ।
ॐ शान्तिः शान्तिः शान्तिः ॥

Asato mā sad gamaya
Tamaso mā jyotir gamaya
Mrtyor mā amrtam gamaya
Om shanti shanti shanti hi

Lead me from falsehood to truth,
Lead me from darkness to light,
Lead me from death to the immortality
Om, Peace, Peace, Peace

H.V. Bhatt

This book is dedicated to my parents,
Rajguru Shri Ichhanath Bhatt
and Srimati Mathuradevi Bhatt.
Your childhood lessons on
Sanatan Dharma have enlightened
and illuminated all walks of my life.

H.V. Bhatt

CONTENTS

Acknowledgments   i

Introduction   1

1 Origins & Beliefs

Ancient Civilization   Pg 5

Space & Time   Pg 15

Planet & Stars   Pg 22

2 Life & Society

Birth   Pg 32

Household   Pg 40

Marriage   Pg 50

Death   Pg 62

3 Worship, Rituals & Festivities

Worship   Pg 68

Rituals & Festivities   Pg 88

4 Past, Present & Future

Ancient Knowledge   Pg 107

Ethics & Politics   Pg 115

Space Age   Pg 138

H.V. Bhatt

INTRODUCTION

These past few years, I have found myself talking to the younger lot in my family, including my son, about my father's legacy, especially his views and knowledge of Hindu dharma, and how it has shaped my own understanding of human societies. This book is an attempt to address some of their persisting anxieties and answer some of their queries to further their understanding of Hindu rituals, practices and references.

In the age of Wikipedia and the Internet, we have access to an explosion of information. However, it's hard to achieve clarity or knowledge without arriving at the rationale behind the rituals of human societies through such information or ready-made knowledge available for instant consumption on the Internet. What is needed is the science behind the timeless wisdom, lessons, or modes of being and understanding. In the science and technology-driven world that we find ourselves living in, *logic* has become the predominant mode of computing or thinking about every question, big or small. The computer-generation mindset looks for logic everywhere. At the first instance, if logic is beyond grasp, the information either stands rejected or ignored in loose comments or jokes.

I welcome this trend as a good shift in our approach to religion. If we are able to logically explain the rationale behind religious practice or beliefs to the new generation, superficial or blind faith could turn into an illuminating or permanent belief system and correct practice. The correct understanding of the religion is necessary for the believers to achieve a comfortable life under all circumstances. No tree can survive long if its roots aren't deeply rooted. Any knowledge imparted forcefully on the young generation will die its own death in the coming time if its roots aren't firmly planted. I believe ethose who desire to acquire knowledge must adhere to the following channel or order of thinking:

1. Anxiety
2. Expectation
3. Exploration
4. Healing
5. Patience

The five stages of acquiring knowledge work as standard operating procedures (SOP) for finding an answer to any question we have. In simple words, if you need to know anything, you need to have enough fire in your mind. The fire needs to be regulated or channelized to find an answer to the anxiety with expected results. Once the desired outcome is in sight, you work on self-regulated questions to make further progress. All undesired points are considered, and substantiating logical conclusion attached to each of the question you have in mind. After considering possible odds and outcomes, we need to have patience till we are clear from all doubts.

Unless we follow a proper school of learning, the answers to our questions can be wrong and unacceptable. aAny particular group or class of people in our society who do not find logical answers to the prevalent rituals of the day eventually stop following those practices.

Indian rishi-munies — the scholars and scientists of their

time — researched and understood how the world works thousands of years ago – a time before the written word was even invented. Oral culture of learning through shloks and stories was dominant in the Hindu religion for a long time. Oral knowledge has more potential to be corrupted and get completely lost. There's a game called telephone where just a small group of people whisper a word into another's ear and this person has to pass on this word into the next person through whispers. As the chain goes on and the word comes back to the originator, chances are it's the wrong word. This happens just within a small group of people within minutes. Imagine how the realms of knowledge would have been corrupted and lost over centuries and across millions of people. Modern science for that matter has been recorded through the written word. It can be consumed perfectly as it was meant to be. That's the reason it has been passed down perfectly in recent generations. But that doesn't mean what the rishi-munies knew was wrong. It has just been lost and at times rediscovered.

This book has been written in the form of questions and answers to help the younger generation understand the logic behind our religious practices. No one should follow a religion blindly. Through this book, I hope they would learn to understand and follow the Hindu religion from their hearts and minds, and help better and improve the quality of life at home and outside.

I thank Mansi, Avani, Sumit for prompting questions included in this book about our ancient heritage and faith. I thank Abhishek for compiling and motivating me to write the answers in form of a book. I would also like to thank my editor Salik Shah for taking this journey with me. His inputs and encouragement has made this a far better book for the readers.

I. Origins & Beliefs

Ancient Civilization

1. What is the meaning of the word 'Hindu'? Who is a Hindu?

The term 'Hindu' was given by foreigners to people who lived across the Indus River. The invaders came from the western part of Indian territories, crossed the river and entered the land, and called it India. When they pronounced 'in,' it sounded like 'hin.' Thus the people living beyond Indus River (i.e., Hindus River, according to them) came to be known as Hindus after the river.

The Hindu religion is originally known as Sanatan Dharma, and the philosophy attached to is *Sarva Dharam Sambhav* — all religions in the world are entitled to enjoy equal status and respect. I will go a step further and say Sanatan Dharma is the mother of all world religions that have adopted some or the other philosophy from Sanatan Dharma, whether Christianity, Islam, Buddhism, Jainism or Sikhism. Each religion has assimilated our teachings in a manner that suits their own people, culture and environment.

2. Where did the Hindus come from? Is Aryan invasion theory correct? How plausible is out-of-India theory, which claims that the early humans came from Africa and spread via India to the rest of the world?

Aryans are mentioned in the *Rigveda*, the oldest scripture of Hinduism, which is also one of the oldest scriptures on humanity and human science in the world. There are many theories on the Aryan origin—from Iran to Northern Europe and India. The Sanskrit meaning of 'Aryan' is 'nobility.' Nobleness is related to culture, and culture is related to education. In a way, the sense of nobleness comes from Sanskar. The nobleness of an individual isn't enough; the nobleness of a group of people is important to be Aryans.

Sanskrit is the oldest language of the world. It is the mother of all the international languages. Its Indian origin makes us realize that India was the center of knowledge. People from all across the globe came to India to learn and acquire knowledges. Some of the people, who came from Europe, Middle East via Iran, Afghanistan and Sindh, settled in India while others returned to their homes. Those who were educated in Vedic sciences and philosophy were referred to and identified as Aryans.

In the 19th century, the word 'Aryan' became popular by its use or misuse in Germany, Northern Europe and Iran. They referred themselves as Aryans, and claimed their ancestors were the ones to introduce Vedic sciences and knowledge to the people on the Indian peninsula. Many historians have given different origin stories of the people of India. I am not claiming or favoring any of the theories. To be an Aryan is to be well-read, educated and cultured, and India was the center of culture, science and education which made nobility its central character and identity.

Once you have a basic knowledge of the Vedas and Upanishads, and familiarity with the Sanskrit language, it will be easy for all Hindus to recognize all the contributions we have made to the world. We lost the glory and knowledge of our past when we stopped learning our own language. Most of us rely upon the opinions of so-called erudite people. They may be familiar with the existing books and commentaries about Sanatan Dharma, but that doesn't give them a right to comment without reading the Vedas and Upanishads. To illustrate a point, Dashavatara of Vishnu tells the whole story of the evolution of mankind from fish to man, but we choose to believe in the most recent theory of evolution, the journey from apes to man!

3. What is the purpose of life according to Hinduism?

The purpose of life is to achieve Moksha. Moksha has many meanings. Every birth is for a purpose; no one in this world is born without any purpose. You are here to perform karma, and contribute to the society the best you can. We live in the modern age of health, security and prosperity because those before us made it possible. Now it is our turn to contribute and build a better world for the generation to come. This is the most practical purpose of life.

You are here to complete some incomplete tasks from your previous birth. As we don't fknow exactly what tasks remain, we commit errors or can't complete all of themrs. This gets added to our account of karma as liability. One takes birth to balance the difference in credits and liability.

In the Garuda Purana, an account of dos and don'ts is clearly stated. In brief, one must walk on the path to moksha by taking into account all of the following:

1. Perfection: One must create perfection in life. We must control our actions and minimize variations. This is a step forward to Moksha.
2. Truthful: We may be right or wrong, but if we are truthful, it doesn't make a difference. Never ever be un-truthful to oneself or the world.
3. Service: Respect every creation (jeev) of God, and serve the needy and the poor, known or unknown. This will give you confidence to be near God.)
4. Ahimsa (Non-Violence): Practice ahimsa to eliminate guilt and feel closer to God.
5. Bhakti: Meditate to control your emotions and connect to the almighty.
6. Peace: ykPray for truth and guidance from dark to light, from fear of death to amrut — eternal life— and peace, only peace.
7. Commitment: Understand your roles and responsibili-

ties, and keep performing them with commitment.

This is moksha and the purpose of life as per Hinduism.

4. What is the logic behind the idea of rebirth? ?

This is a tsimple yet profound question raised by followers of nearly all major religions. New researches and investigations are undertaken in every generation to shed new light on the question. Many great poets, philosophers and authors have attempted to answer this question in not just one book, but a series of books and volumes. Still the question remains unanswered to everyone's satisfaction.

We need to approach this question from a different angle. First, we need to understand the theory of rebirth. The total human population is seven billion today. No one has ever seen God, but most people believe that there is something like God. Second, the holy prophets of major religions — Lord Ram, Krishna, Jesus Christ and Mohammad — took birth in their respective land, region and country, not in overlapping places. The definition of 'god; depends upon time and people, and their immediate needs and understandings.

The process of creation, resistance, assimilation, crisis, and rebirth of many new branches of a religion continues even today. Every religion defines 'god' in their own ways; the religious gurus define rules and practices as per spiritual or social need of their age and environment. And they make these rules and practices simple and compelling enough for every class of people, irrespective of their education or level of intelligence. Some individuals and communities blindly adopt their preachings, while others challenge. Those who challenge a faith or its beliefs end up creating their own set of beliefs and practices.

The theory of rebirth is based on the law of karma. According to the law of karma, if you commit a crime, or engage in wrong, violent or unethical work in your present life, you may have to face the consequences in your next birth. Likewise, you will be rewarded for any good work or service you do today in your next birth.

What is this next birth? In my opinion, the next birth is our next moment, next day, next year or next decade.

If you harm someone, he may accept the injury or defeat today, but he would certainly make preparations to avenge the injury or defeat tomorrow. So even if you have won today, tomorrow may not be the same. The cycle continues without an end: for every action, there is a reaction. There is no escape from engagement, worry or uncertainty. This is the meaning of the theory of rebirth. Our present is the result of our past, and today is the seed of tomorrow. This is the cycle of life after life. It binds everyone — individual, family, society, country and the entire world. Good work brings its rewards, and bad karma comes with terrible consequences. You'll reap what you sow, whether in this life or the next.

5. Can you describe Hinduism in a few words?

Hinduism is part of Sanatan Dharma, which is one of the oldest religious philosophies in the world based on Vedic research. Vedas are the oldest form of all sciences: astrology, mathematics, social sciences, politics, management, and law. What we know today is available in the Vedas in some form or the other. It is said that Vedas were written by the gods. No one knows who wrote them. In the Vedic age, most education was oral. Any existing body of knowledge was shared by Rishi-Munis with their disciples in their ashrams orally. Over a period of time, their teachings were slowly documented. What we read today is not the original form of the text, but documented thousands of years later by various scholars. For example, Lord Ram was born about 10,000 years ago, and Krishna around 5,000 years ago. The books about the two, Ramayana and Mahabharata, were written by Valmiki and Ved Vyas respectively about 2,000 years later.

We should be thankful to the Rishis-Munis for their work in writing down the present form of our religious texts. I believe these texts were written to help the common man understand the basic principles of Vedas. Each and every character in these books represent a type of personality whose story illustrates the consequences of good and bad karma in one's life. There is something to learn from each of these characters and stories.

Two thousand years ago, Shankaracharya was born. Scholars and gurus have been delivering these lectures and the Katha since then. Every time someone listens to them, there is a scope for new interpretation. One feels that the teachings of Vedas are true even today. Everybody feels that he or she is connected to them. This is the beauty of these texts.

I will try to explain this aspect in more detail in my next book which will be based on my own experiments through religious principles on Management.

In its simplest form, I will define the uniqueness of Hinduism through these four principles:

1. Whatever happens had to happen that way, whether birth, growth or development, even sickness and death.
2. Whoever you meet in life, you were destined to meet. There is a purpose in meeting that person in your life. S/he has come to you either to pay or receive, teach or learn, take or give.
3. Whatever will happen will happen at its own time. Do not hurry to get everything you want. Keep working, and you'll reach your goal in its own time.
4. What is over is over. Do not hold on to the past. Move ahead in life without regrets. What is over is over, and you cannot do anything about it. Let us not carry any guilt. Keep moving.

These are the four basic principles of life that I have been taught and followed.

I have tried to explain these core ideas of Hinduism in plain words for the benefit of the common man, and if it helps families to enjoy its fruits, this book would have served its purpose. In absence of any such documentation, people tend to ignore their religion, and it is quite possible that over a period due to discontentment, it would die and people wouldn't even know what they lost.

In the upcoming book, I will explain the principles of modern management based on Hinduism to help small entrepreneurs find success in the increasingly competitive world.

Space & Time

6. What is the Hindu theory of mankind's evolution?

The Hindu theory of mankind's evolution can be found in the stories of Dashavatara. The word "dashavatara" is derived from two words, 'dash; (ten) and 'avatar' (incarnation), and refers to the ten births of Lord Vishnu, who is supposed to manage the universe. The stories of his ten avatars hold clues to how different species on water and earth came into being.

Let me briefly explain the ten avatars of Lord Vishnu and their meanings below:

1. Matsya (The Fish): Lord Vishnu first took birth in this universe as a fish, which is also the first creature on the planet. This story tells us how the first human Manu was saved by this Matsya avatar, which represents jeev or life.

2. Kurma (The Giant Tortoise): Kurna provided the base for a heavy mountain used for churning of the sea to produce amrit (the nectar of immortality). This represents the enduring longevity of the human species on the back of a tortoise, which is very strong and lives long.

3. Varaha (The Boar): The battle between Hiranyaksha and Varaha went on for a thousand years. Lord Vishnu took the birth as Varaha and took out the earth from the bottom of the cosmic ocean between his tusks and placed it in the universe. When the Varaha brought out the earth on his tusks, the earth was round—it's likely that our ancestors knew about its shape even then.

4. Narasimha (The Man-Lion): The unruly king Hiranyakashipu couldn't be killed by a human or an animal either during day or night. Lord Vishnu took Narasimha avatar and killed him with his hands. This was the time where the principles of social justice and leadership by right people were introduced in the social life.

5.   Vamana (The Dwarf): King Bali with his devotion and penance organized a Yagna and to take over the command from the king of Devas, Indra. The worried Devas requested Lord Vishnu to save them from Bali. Lord Vishnu took the avatar of a child-like Brahmin and went to Bali and asked for an area of land equal to his three footsteps. King Bali agreed, and the Vaman put one step on earth, second on the sky, and asked for the place to put his third step. The king requested him to put it on his head. And the lord made him the king of patal lok, or underground world. This story warns against the dangers of excessive ambitions in all forms, and conveys that one's right place is in the hands or the feet of the lord. This represented an era of set rules and expectations of dharma from the ruler.

6.   Parshuram (The Warriore): Parshuram was the son of a Brahmin father and Kshtariya mother. When Parshuram offered milk to a ruler who had come to his ashram, the king tried to take his magical cow, Kamdhenu, by force. The saint refused, and the king destroyed his ashram. The angry saint then destroyed the entire community of Kshatriya 21 times. This represented an era where Guru had the knowledge but didn't use it for his selfish gains or power.

7.   Rama: Lord Rama was also an avatar of Lord Vishnu. He took birth in the house of King Dasharath to restore dharma in the society. In the Rama avatar, we see the ideal king. He was a noble, polite and self-sacrificing king, who valued and adopted a true democratic way to rule a nation. The common man even today talk about Ram-rajya. We must feel proud of this avatar, who has become a symbol of the democratic form of governance in the world.

8.   Krishna: Krishna is one of the most fascinating avatars of Lord Vishnu. His mission was to finish all Rakshasa right from his childhood. He took birth in a prison, and killed Kali Naag as a boy. He killed Putna the devil, and the

Kans, the sinful ruler and his own maternal uncle. He also secured love of Gopis, friendship of Sudama. He was the Guru of Arjuna, an advisor to all Pandavas, a mentor and a fighter for the just cause. He showed all the qualities of a good leader in a developed society.

9. Balrama / Buddha (the Peace and Ahimsa): In this avatar, the lord displayed the importance of Ahimsa and proved that the war is not always the right solution. Peace and coexistence is more important. Balram's main tool was the hal (plough) for agriculture. We can use technology to irrigate land to grow fruits and vegetables, and various crops to sustain life — that was Balrama's message. Now the world needs more technological development to feed its population, and it was started by Balaram.

10. Kalki: We all are living in an era of technology and science, good and bad, wars and conflict. The material needs of the society will lead to distrust and confusions, violence and hatred. The world will die its own death, and it'll be rebuilt by this Kalyuga avatar of Lord Vishnu.

The theory of ten avatars show the evolution of life, mankind, and its complex codes and systems that gave birth to our civilization. At the same time, it also warns us of its eventual downfall, followed by a cycle of regeneration.

7. Why is the statue of Hindu god, Nataraja, at CERN, Geneva?

The creation of the universe is still a mystery. rReligious, social and political codes were developed to enable quality of life here on Earth. Yet we remain unsatisfied. The Sanatan Dharma contains within it the science and art of living and dying. This is the need of the hour.

The European Organization for Nuclear Research known as CERN was formed in late 20th century to unravel the mystery of the universe down to its basic building block —atom. How was it formed? How does it operate? Who runs it? The Vedic scholars have answered some of these questions accurately, and m odern science is only beginning to acknowledge their achievement and contribution. CERN is a step in the right direction to connect the missing links and establish the facts.

Rishi Kanada (popularly known as Kashyapa) had given a theory of atom some 2,500 years ago. He mentioned that these atoms are present in the environment but not visible to the naked eye. He developed the theory of molecule for the first time in the history of chemistry. His understanding and teachings were similar to modern scientists. This makes me believe that Indian scientists will make great contributions to the CERN project and the world in years to come.

The Nataraj statue placed at the CERN's main office is a gift from the Indian Government. India is one of the member countries of the CERN, which is npaying an homage to the Vedic knowledge and its continued relevance through the dancing idol of Shiva, the god of creation and destruction.

8. What are the four Yugas? In which eon are we living? Why does it matter?

As per Sanatan Dharma, there are four Yugas:

1. Sat Yuga: eIn the perfect age of Sat Yuga, t There was no religion. People were healthy and lived long. People didn't cook, and ate what was given by nature. There was no scarcity, rich or poor, class or creed. Everyone lived happily and peacefully. And there was only one Veda.

2. Treta Yuga: This is the time of the rise of empires and domination of people. People lost health and age. They started farming and mining. This was the time when Lord Rama came to establish the rule of law or dharma on Earth. He was Maryada Pourshottam, whose life was an example to the world for just and proper human conduct.

3. Dvapara Yuga: The Veda was divided into four Vedas during this Yuga. The average age declined further. People weakened, and those who were powerful dominated and preyed on the poor and weak. 'Might is right' became the theory. The population expanded but resources were limited, which led to social inequalities. This was the time when Lord Krishna took birth to set right the things which were against the natural law of survival.

4. Kali Yuga: Today we are living in the age of Kali. People commit sin — crimes — and lack concern for fellow human beings and living creatures. The society is full of manipulators and liars. The ancient knowledge and spirituality have been lost. People eat unhealthy food and become weak, and grow more materialistic than ever. The rule of law shifts from public service to commerce and exploitation. The average life span at the end of this Yuga will be 70 years.

The above division of time is not restricted to stages of human development. It indicates that in each Yuga, God has taken avatar and has guided people to lead better and respectable life. Not everyone adopts religious preachings wholesale. Some object, some reject and some correct themselves — a process that continues to this day from the inception of our universe.

Planets & Stars

9. What is astrology? What role does it play in Hindu religion?

Our body contains elements of the whole universe. In other words, we can say that all ingredients that make up our body are taken from the universe. When we say this, it is obvious that all the stars in the universe have some or the other role in making our body or rather they are present in our body.

The moon controls the human mind; its presence and position around Earth has effects on our mind and soul at a deeper level. In some cases, the effects are direct and intense, sometimes lighter or indirect. The influence of a star's position in the universe has different effects on the different objects.

On full moon days, the lunar gravity swells sea level by six to ten feet. mMental hospitals take extra care of patients on these days as patientsl behave more erratically. eIn legends of werewolves, the transformation happens during full moon — an exaggeration, of course. The mentally-challenged person loses the balance of mind, whereas a normal person is able to control it despite the lunar pull.

The position of stars determine the effect they have upon people, big or small. The old Hindu scholars intensely studied the effects of stars on human beings and developed guidelines to benefit from them. Over centuries, the knowledge was lost or corrupted, and misunderstandings arose in subsequent generations.

An astrologer first needs to identify the problem, do a root-cause analysis, suggest mantras, advise on fasting and if necessary suggest stones one could wear. Make an SOP to be followed, set a direction to focus efforts, and achieve desired results. This is what happens in medical science. The patient tells his problems to a doctor, and the doctor examines and studies the symptoms, advises medicines and appropriate food, do's and don'ts, and only if necessary, goes for something invasive like an operation. Same is true in case of an astrologer too. One does not go for a drastic measure without proper understanding.

10. What are the days of the week according to the Hindu calendar?

The Hindu religion is the world's oldest religion. We can trace the influence of Indian astronomy on naming of days across the globe, including Gregorian calendar. Some scholars claim that zodiac and naming system of Hindu astrology likely developed in the centuries following the arrival of Greek astrology with Alexander the Great in 326 BC.

1. According to the Hindu calendar, the first day of the week is Ravivar. 'Ravi' means the Sun, and 'var' means 'day.' In Gregorian calendar, the first day of the week is also named after the sun i.e. Sunday.

2. The second day of the week is Somvar. Here, 'Som' means Lord Shiva. Shiva has Chandra on his head. We also call this Chandravar — the moon day or Monday.

3. The third day of the week is Mangalvar. 'Mangal' means Mars. In the English calendar, it's Tuesday. The word 'Tues' is derived from 'Tiw,' which is equated with Mars in *interpretatio germanica* – a practice of Germanic peoples of identifying foreign Gods as members of their own pantheon.

4. The fourth day of the week is Budhvar, or Wednesday. In Hindu astronomy, 'Budh' represents Mercury. The word Wednesday is also associated with Mercury.

5. Thursday is called Guruwar in Hindu religion. 'Guru' represents Jupiter. In pre-Christian days, the word 'thus' represented Jupiter.

6. Next comes Shukravar, or Friday, both is named after Venus.

7. The last day of the week is Shanivar, or Saturday, both

named after Saturn.

The Hindu religion has influenced all world religionsd. Who is credited for advancement in science, religion and philosophy depends on the dominant religion or society of the day. That's the way the world works but my hope is that we would dig deeper to understand our history better.

11. Why do people wear rings with various stones on their fingers? What is the science behind the use of such stones?

Indian astronomy occupies a glorious position in the history of sciences; it continues to influence and play an important role in the rise of modern science. According to Hindu beliefs, our body is made of five basic elements (panch mahabhoot):

1. Prithvi (Earth): This represents matter that make our flesh, bones and organs.
2. Akash (Sky): This represents our brain, intelligence or quality of mind. What type of attitude, thinking or analytical power do we possess is determined by this element.
3. Jal (Water): Water is life. Our body is made of 50-65% water according to modern science.
4. Agni (Fire): Our body generates heat and fire, and its very presence in the body makes us alive. Extinguish the heat, and we're dead.
5. Vayu (Air): We breathe oxygen and exhale carbon dioxide, maintaining the balance of life and nature.

Our body starts development right from the womb. Based on the astronomical conditions and their effects, our body starts responding to the environment in subtle ways and takes its final form. The astrologer studies the powerful and weak influences upon our personality, and recommends us ways to counter or strengthen these influences and factors for our peace of mind, welfare and growth. Based on the color and healing properties of specific stones, the astrologer chooses the right stones for us depending on our needs and requirements. We wear specific stones on our fingers to keep the astrologer's insight and advice for improvement in sight and mind.

It is worth remembering that astrological advice is not destiny — it can only shed light on the human condition, and point us to the right course of direction or solution. Over time people have been misguided and taken their advice as fate or destiny, which is deeply troubling. The correct understanding of the ancient science could benefit both advisor and advisee.

In Hindu astrology, there are seven physical planets and two shadow planets. Each day of the week is allotted to one physical planet. These are Sun, Moon, Mars, Mercury, Jupiter, Venus and Saturn. All these planets have direct or indirect effect on us. Based on their positioning at the time of one's birth, a Kundali (birth chart) is made. As per stars' movement, their effects are calculated by an astrologer, and advice is given to take care of the effects on one's mind and body.

It's not scientifically proven yet, but there are some facts which we can look into before we discard astrology totally. The movement of planet was accurately calculated by astrologers of the yore much before modern science. The knowledge of eclipse has been there for centuries in Hinduism. Mars has been known as the red planet in Indian astrology for centuries — a claim NASA validated in 1965. The predictions made by an astrologer may be not completely correct but the temperament of a person is largely correct.

There is some science behind astrology, but due to the lack of knowledge or corruption of perfect knowledge, the interpretations are misguided. Maybe someday we might rediscover or understand the exact science of effects planets and stars have on us.

e s t   tm .

12. What are the importances of Full Moon (Poonam) and No Moon Day (Amavasya)?

The appearance of moon in different shapes and sizes seems normal today. When there was no scientific explanation or knowledge about it, this caused much anxiety and superstition among common folks. The Hindu rishi-munies have carefully studied, calculated and predicted the moon's changing shapes, its movement, and their effects on human beings.

The full moon day is the day of complete mental strength, while it's best to avoid dangerous tools on no moon days since our mental abilities are somewhat dull.

There is a ritual to observe Chandra darshan after Amavasya. This marks the start of a new month. The darshan has a ritual to have a new wish for the month. This is nothing but fixing our agenda for the next month. On Amavasya, the last day of the month, there is a ritual to donate something to the needy people. It helps to take stock of our month, be thankful and give back to society.

13. What is 'Muhurt' and why it is so important in performing religious functions?

As per Vikram Sambat, the Hindu calendar, the new Year is Chaitra mas (month). Each month has two fortnights called Shulka Paksh and Krishna Paksh. Each fortnight has 15 days (tithi). Each month has one full moon day (Poonam) and one no moon day (amavasya). There are repeat days and reduced days in each of the fortnight: vraddhi and kshati tithi. The day is not calculated based on day and night but the movement of our moon and visible stars.

A professional astrologer can determine the right day and time for an important work or function. Certain star positions are not shubh or favorable and need to be ignored. If the adverse shadow or alignment of the planet and stars can be avoided, there is more chances of success. However, it doesn't mean that you cannot perform an auspicious function if there are no favorable alignment. We can perform or begin work on a good project at any time.

In today's parlance, "Muhurt" allows us to book the priest for the function, otherwise he may have other tasks or patrons to attend to on that day.

II. Life & Society

Birth

14. What is the importance of god-bhari, the baby shower ceremony?

This is one of the sixteen Sanskars in Hindu religion. It is an important turning point for both man and woman. Being a father or a mother is an unforgettable experience. The god-bhari pooja is to acquire blessings of all Hindu gods and one's ancestors. The pandit ji (priest) who helps perform the pooja makes us feel that we are directly taking blessings from God.

This puja makes the society aware about the arrival of a new member in the family. During the ceremony, close relatives offer dry fruits and grains to the pregnant woman to make her realize that proper care and nutrition is a must for her. She leaves her husband's house and goes to her parent's house till the birth of child as she is likely to be more comfortable with her own family members and her home. In old days, deliveries were managed at home by midwives. There were no hospitals. So in a way this ceremony also serves as a notice for the house to be kept clean and everything in order.

Offering good clothes, ornaments and gift motivates the mother to acquire a special status in the society. She gets psychologically and mentally ready to face the pain of labor. Generally, this ritual is performed at the completion of seven months of pregnancy. Thereafter the woman goes to her parent's house. The mother must remain away from her husband for her and her child's safety during the pregnancy. Modern science also advises against intercourse in the last trimester.

15. Why don't Hindus allow haircut of an infant until the age of three?

The skull of a newborn child is very soft and fragile. It takes time for bones to develop completely. Haircutting tools are dangerously sharp or pointed. Any mishandling of razors, scissors or electronic tools could cause serious damage to the head, whether you're a grownup or an infant.

There is another reason: long hair can be easily combed. When the grown hair is pulled by the comb, it exerts pressure on the skull, which increases blood circulation in the area that allows for the skull to develop well.

The barber doesn't work for you alone. He works for many people. The haircutting tools like blade and scissor could be infected, and if a child's immune system is not strong enough, this may be a deadly combination. Keeping all this in mind, it is advised to cut hair after the child reaches the age of three, and in the presence of senior members of the family.

In old days, it was customary to wear a turban. In the West, people wore hat. We find suggestion to cover one's head in all religions and parts of the world. This is directly related to the safety of the head.

16. What is the reason behind our ear-piercing ceremony?

Wearing of ornaments is common among boys and girls in India — a tradition possibly as old as the Indian civilization. Piercing is done at an early age, when the child is young, as it's easy and safe to puncture the tender skine. All relatives present at the ceremony give blessings and good wishes to the child. They wear rich ornaments, and also present some ornaments as good wishes.

There are a few more reasons for this ceremony. Not so long ago, our elders and teachers used to pull our ears if we did not answer their questions correctly. And if we committed a mistake and wish to seek forgiveness, we would touch our ears and apologize.

Crossing the hands while pulling ears during simple exercises like stand up, sit down may sharpen our mind. There is a vein passing through the top and bottom of the ear to the brain; it is believed that puncturing this vein helps to control anger and depression.

17. Why is the newborn child given silver utensils by their relatives?

In our day to day life we use many utensils for various purposes: cooking, serving, eating. We have used various metals to make utensils over the years: copper, brass, silver, Panch Dhatu, Kansa, etc. These days we have started using stainless steel utensils as well.

Silver has been considered a purest metal since generations. It has been a metal for upper classes in the society. It's valued for its purity and non-infection qualities. Science has proven that silver is a bacteria-free metal. Furthermore, this metal has no reaction with milk, curd, juice etc. which we often give to the newborn. Hence it is the most desirable metal for utensils used to feed children.

The newborn is offered silver utensils by close relatives as marks of love and care. This is also given for the first child in the family, so that subsequent children can also use them. So while it is a lovely custom that people follow, it's important to know its benefits as well.

18. What is Yagnopavit (Janeu) ceremony?

As per Hindu religion, a person passes through 16 Sanskars (learnings) in a lifetime. This starts from garbha dharan (pregnancy) to antim-sanskar (death and cremation). Yagnopavit (thread ceremony) is one of the 16 Sanskars a Hindu is supposed to acquire. After this Sanskar, a person wears the Janeu (holy thread) on his body for a lifetime. These days, it has become more of a ritual or ceremony where people gather, celebrate and then return to their homes. The person who is given this Janeu removes the thread after some time, and all is back to normal.

This ceremony is held to mark the start of a life of the student after early education imparted by parents at home. Now the young boy has to leave the house and stay at an ashram under a guru. His head is shaven, and he is given simple clothing, a stick and books. This ceremony is as much for the child or the student as for his parents and close relatives. The elders must let the student go to acquire education and knowledge, and become a good human being.

The shaven head makes the student focus on studies and not appearance. The stick is for self defense, and the loose clothing for ease. After the thread ceremony, the batuk runs and the maternal uncle tries to catch, carry and bring him back to his parents. This ceremony has a message that the batuk is so excited to gain knowledge that he runs to the ashram. The maternal uncle (Mama) runs after him to catch him and bring him back out of love. But later, they allow him to go with a promise that at the time of marriage, the uncle will meet him again and bring him good clothing.

This ceremony is full of love, excitement and commitment. The person hereafter has to lead a disciplined life and concentrate on making himself a good knowledgeable person and a good human being to take charge from his seniors once he is back home.

This ceremony is usually performed in the Brahmin community. However, this has nothing to do with Brahmins. A person becomes Brahmin only after acquiring knowledge. A Brahmin doesn't become a brahmin from birth; he becomes Brahmin only after Yagnopavit Sanskars.

The Hindu society is divided into four classes of people: Brahmins (priests, scholars and teachers), Kshatriyas (rulers, warriors and administrators), Vaishyas (agriculturalists and merchants), and Shudras (laborers and service providers). It is assumed that only Brahmin is supposed to acquire knowledge, and hence this Sanskar is given only to Brahmin. However, this ceremony is supposed to be followed by all Hindus whose children seek education under the guidance of a guru or a teacher.

During this ceremony, the guru whispers and gives Gayatri Mantra to the student while covering their heads with a piece of cloth. Why is this mantra given in confidentiality? Knowledge acquired or employed without competency or confidentiality may result in disaster. This is what is happening today. Weapons like guns, AK47s, rocket launchers and missiles have reached the hands of incompetent and dangerous men, including terrorists, and they use these weapons to harm people, animals, and nature without understanding, shame or regret.

There's a story in Mahabharata about Dronacharya and Eklavya. When Eklavya sealed the mouth of a dog with arrows without harming the creature, Dronacharya and his pupils were shocked. How could a tribal boy acquire such skills? Upon further inquiry, it was revealed that the boy had mastered his skills by watching Dronacharya's teachings to Arjun from behind a tree. As a teacher of the royal princes, Dronacharya couldn't permit this—he asked Eklavya for his thumb as Guru-Daxina, and Eklavya chopped it off and gave it to him. This story illustrates the principle of acquiring five competencies or Ws before one H: What, Why, When, Where, Who – thereafter comes How. If How is acquired before 5 W, there is a danger in all stages of learning.

In other words, today knowledge is within everyone's reach (like the trigger and fire). But we do not know on whom it should be fired, why it should be fired, and when it should be fired, if at all. These questions are never asked, which has put the society in great danger. We are knowledgeable enough to keep weapons of mass destruction like atom and hydrogen bombs out of the hands of immature people. The Hindu religion teaches us that the terms of confidentiality and competency is vital before knowledge is given or acquired.

Household

19. Why do we perform Vastu Puja? Is this really necessary for the house?

The Vastu Puja is normally performed on occupying a new house to make the area worth living. The Yagna is performed to clean the environment, and get rid of any bad influence or atmosphere. The earth on which you have constructed your house is as old as the universe. Before it was occupied, the land was bare, agricultural, or even a forest. Under all these conditions, the land is supposed to be exposed to non-living conditions. This land is purified and made habitable through the puja. The fire and the smoke from various yagna ingredients make the environment free from germs and bacteria, and make it healthy for people to move in.

Vastu Puja helps fulfill the following requirements:

- Anyone living residing before you will be respectfully requested to depart.
- Opportunity to receive blessings from the almighty to build a happy home.
- The new location is known to relatives and friends who are invited to the function.
- Spreading the sut (cotton) thread around your house helps people to learn the area of the house.
- Social value is attached to the owner.

20. Why is it customary to touch feet of elders and priests?

As we grow old, we add not only years to our lives but also experience and wisdom. There are many stages in one lifetime: infancy, childhood, teenage, youth, adult, middle age, retirement and old age. We keep accumulating noticeable and unnoticeable, recordable and unreportable experiences. If we sit back and recollect all these experiences, we will not be able to remember everything that has been gained or registered perfectly. However, some of these memories resurface at times of need to help us deal with the problem or situation at hand. This is nothing but insight from your experience.

In Hindu society, there is a special place for old and experienced people. Elders slowly acquire the advisor's role to help and guide young people toward progress. Acharya Chanakya has said it is not necessary to do everything all by yourself, learn from others and others' mistakes. You need not repeat all that was done in the past — learn from others' mistakes. If you try to do all that was done in past, this life will be insufficient to achieve new landmarks. To learn and accomplish new things, you need an experienced guide – the senior members of your family and society. In the present world, they are also known as consultants. Someone who is able to see you from different angles, and use all of his knowledge and experience to guide you.

When you bow to someone, you show respect towards the person, and the other person experiences recognition of his knowledge and age. When these two things happen simultaneously, the right environment is created for the transfer of knowledge, giving and taking, guru and shishya. That said, this custom should not be forced upon anyone. If you feel naturally inclined to bow down to the knowledgeable and saints, you should not hold yourself back or let ego take over. A sincere bow is always returned with heartfelt blessings.

21. Why is it customary to press elders' legs?

As a person grows older, blood circulation in his or her body becomes slow and hampers day to day activity. Stiffness and joint pains become regular. Our heart is located in the upper chest of the body. Our legs are down. Blood circulates from heart to all parts of our body, and the legs are far off from the heart. The heart has to pump the blood more forcefully to reach the legs.

As the heart grows old with our age, it affects our blood circulation. Old people do not get proper sleep, and keep struggling if they are all by themselves. Pressing or massaging legs of old people indirectly helps their heart as now it has to work a little less to aid better blood circulation. This gives comfort to body. There is also a psychological reason behind this practice. Feeling better as the result of the massage, old people will initiate talks, and you will be benefited by this conversation if you take it in the right spirit. This whole act creates a conducive environment to converse, bond and learn.

It is an old tradition. Now massaging hands have been replaced by machines and Ortho chairs. What's missing is the knowledge sharing which happened with the younger ones, a sense of bonding.

22. Why should you sleep with your head facing south?

In a working compass, the needle always faces north. There are magnetic waves on the north, and that is how we can easily identify rest of the directions: south, east and west.

The earth's magnetic waves keep working endlessly, every minute and each second. Within our bodies, micro metallic particles circulate continuously through the blood. If we sleep facing north, the micro metallic particles in our body may get stuck in the brain and prevent blood circulations in the brain, which could either affect restlessness or mental disorder over a period of time. Contrary to that, the particles will move out of skull / brain and move to our legs where they can be managed without any major problem.

Only the dead bodies are kept with their skull facing north with the hope of activating the brain to the extent possible and return to life.

23. Why do Hindus sit on the ground to have meal?

The average human body temperature is around 38 degree celsius. The food we take is often around 22 to 26 degree celsius. When we eat, our body shifts and redistributes heat from other parts of the body to the area around our stomach. By sitting on the ground, we partially block the main vein, which passes to our legs through hips. This way the blood going to legs remains limited to its minimal requirement. The surplus blood accumulates around our stomach. Our blood is both a power-generating plant, and a heat distribution mechanism. When we sit to eat, the food is heated, and it helps in timely digestion. If the heat is not supplied in time, the food in our body will be spoiled by fermentation and could create digestive problems.

The best way to eat is by sitting on the groundl. If this is not possible, sit on a chair.

24. Why do we take spicy meal in the beginning and sweet in the end?

When we eat, the acid formation in the stomach is at its peak, which helps quicken digestion. If the stimulation of digestive glands do not act quickly, the food start will degrade and ferment, which could lead to acidity. Sweet food contains alkaline substances which subside excessive acid formation. It balances the acid to the extent needed.

Hindus have nearly perfect meal practices. We take food in a very balanced way — we start with rice, which is full of starch but soft to the walls of our stomach. In the beginning of the meal, soft and excessive acid blend. At the end, the sweet cleans the spicy food from our mouth. This way you do not need water to gulp. This is very important since we should not take water immediately after the food. This regulates the heat and keeps digestion stable in the stomach.

25. Why do elders offer curd and gud (jaggery) to the young who are about to head out for an important work or mission?

Whenever we go out for an important task or a mission, the senior members in our family offer gud and dahi. It is a way to remind you what attitude or qualities are necessary to achieve success or complete the mission.

Milk is natural but the curd is man-made. When you face people in the world, you should present as 'made' and not 'born.' You must prove and demonstrate that you have acquired the knowledge and expertise necessary for success. The curd is the disintegrated part of milk. The one going out of the house on the specific mission must, for the time being, detach him/herself from the house and focus on the mission.

Gud helps you keep your tongue sweet. Be kind, positive and sweet in presence of others in order to achieve success.

Whenever you are out to complete a specific work, forget your house and concerns, and concentrate on the mission and keep your tongue sweet. Both gud and curd are full of nutritious value, and good for one's health, and you shouldn't be any less. Your attitude, presence and contribution to the society should be positive, healthy and beneficial to yourself and others.

26. Why do we offer milk with gud/sugar when welcoming a person into the house?

Like we offer gud and dahi to a person going out, we offer milk with sugar to the person coming to our house.

Milk is a sign of power and strength. Anyone coming to our home could be tired and exhausted, and s/he needs to regain their strength. The milk and sugar give required strength.

No matter under what circumstances they may have come to your house, it's worth remembering that the guest needs to be like sugar in the milk. Like all family members, they should feel comfortable enough to sweeten and improve the household environment.

If curd is symbol of disintegration, milk is symbol of integration. By offering milk with gud or sugar, we hope to improve the quality of our interactions, time and presence. Unfortunately, we have no time to perform such rituals these days. We are taught to speak straight, brief and to the point. Communication is faster, but not pleasant or perfect anymore. The benefits of keeping the old tradition and message alive in our hearts are immense and vital for improving everyone's life.

27. Why do Hindus observe fasting?

Our body works continuously, uninterruptedly even before the hour of our birth. We inhale oxygen, and it is diluted in the blood, which carries it to all the parts of the body. Food goes to the stomach and turns into energy and transferred to the body to perform our day to day activities. Our body is a processing plant and like all plants it needs rest and repair. The only difference is that an artificial power plant can could go on a planned shutdown, our body cannot.

Our ancestors and Rishi-Munies discovered the perfect SOP (standard operating procedure) to maintain and keep human body fit without a complete shutdown i.e. fasting observed in a disciplined manner. It was embedded in the religion so that the common men and women would take it seriously and follow it. Fasting gives relaxation to the body from the daily routine. Different types of food is allowed to be taken, which has a different role like cleaning, heat balance, and less pressure on digestive organs.

In some cases, complete fasting is advised to either burn extra fat or generate heat to kill unwanted, undesirable bacteria in the body. We must note that it is not always true that what we eat today is excreted out completely the next day. There are some foods that remain in body for one to two weeks and some for even months. When you observe fast, the body consumes this surplus fat and this way the cycle of fat generation and fat burning gets activated faster. Think of fasting as an ancient diet plan akin to what today's nutritionists and dietitians come up with.

There is a ritual that on fasting day our portion of food must be given to other needy people or Brahmins. This is baked in the religion to encourage giving to the society.

Marriage

28. Why does gold play such an important role in a relationship, particularly Hindu marriages?

Gold has an important status across the world. Every nation plans to increase their gold assets. In the gold standard system, a country that prints paper currency has to make sure that they have an equivalent value in gold. This is a metal recognized and traded worldwide and is easily cashable. sWhat is applicable to nations is also applicable to the society at large and small families. Every man looks to stock gold, which turns out to be a good vehicle for investment as well.

In our daily lives, if we get the gift of money we forget the moment it is spent. If we get gift an objectm, we remember it till the thing lasts. If we get clothing, we remember the person who gave us the gift for couple of years. The gift and the person who gave the gift remains in our memory for as long as the gift lasts. We remember gold and silver for a lifetime as we often pass them to the next generation. This is why our near and dear ones give us what we can cherish for life.

Gold is also a practical gift. We have the flexibility of converting it into cash any time in any part of the world.

29. What is meaning of gotra? Why is there restriction to marry within members of the same gotra?

Modern science has concluded that chances of genetic disorders increase in case of children amongst close relatives. Diseases like haemophilia, color blindness, skin diseases, etc are largely due to marriages within one's kins. If the child is born from distant blood relations, the risks to the child's health reduce significantly, and such children grow mentally and physically strong and healthy.

The gotra is named after ancient Rishi-Munies like Bharadwaj Kaudinya, Vashishtha and Krishnatri. The gotras also form surnames like Choudhary, Chouhans, Sisodia, etc. These names in essence help in differentiating groups. The same name represents the same family. This way every Hindu has some or the other gotra attached to his or her family. That has become the identity of the family tree. The Hindus are advised not to marry in the same Gotra i.e. within the same clan or family.

In Hindu marriages, Mangal (Mars) represents the blood in our body, and if there is a Mangalic dosh, then marriage between such a couple isn't advised. It may be noted that Gotra and Mangal dosh are different parameters but both are related to genetic science.

30. What is Vagdan – the half-wedding ritual before a marriage?

Vagdan is known as half marriage. The meaning of 'vag' is vachan or verbal agreement, and 'dan' means an offer. Vagdan is a verbal agreement to a relationship. In olden days the elderly used to go the girl's parents to propose a relationship. Once the relationship was agreed upon, Vagdan was performed by the girl's parents. It is important to point out that the right to accept or reject is in the hands of the girl's family. The boy's parents will go to her home and not the other way round. Mmore importance is given to the girl and her relatives in Hindu marriages.

After the ritual, the couple are allowed enough time and space to get to know and understand each other better. This so-called half marriage can be nullified before the actual marriage if things don't work out, and isn't considered to be a bad thing or a taboo. Until the actual marriage takes place, the couple is on a close watch. If there is any doubt or disagreement, the same may be clarified by either side before the final marriage. It is also customary to have the boy and the girl invited on some special occasion or festival to give a chance to both of them to understand each other better.

In arranged marriages this is important as the boy and the girl do not know each other at all. They need some time to develop an understanding. In the process the parents and other members of the family also get to know each other closely. This is followed in present times as well albeit in a different name and form.

31. Why do we offer gud (jaggery) and dhania (coriander seeds) as soon as the marriage proposal is finalized?

Offering gud and dhaniya is a very old tradition. :In old days, this was a readymade sweet which didn't require any preparation and was instantly available in all households. Offering gud and dhaniya immediately after the agreement of marriage is to start a new relationship with sweet in your mouth. A symbol to keep sweetness of tongue to avoid any sort of misunderstanding and conflict. Gud mixed with coriander is also an indication that in this new relationship, there may be bitterness with sweetness but that's a way of life and we must accept that and stay together through thick and thin.

The old-timers were smart enough to communicate the messages through such rituals. The same is maintained today without a real understanding of the message. If we have a better understanding of the reasoning behind such rituals, it may lead to better relationships that last a lifetime. I appreciate this question by a young family member. Once this is understood, the spirit of ritual is clear and the custom becomes far more effective.

32. Why do the girl's parents wash their son-in-law's feet? What is the significance of such a ritual bordering on insult?

This is a very good question.   In most religions the girl goes to the husband's house after marriage. This is very critical for girls' parents. The child has taken birth in their house, grown up under their guidance, and now all of a sudden, she marries and goes away. This is a big emotional event and concern for any father or mother. They hope the girl would be able to accommodate to the new surroundings and people. Their only hope is the son-in-law — he is expected to manage everything, and take care of her, guide her and make her comfortable. So they worship him like a god, and wash his feet and welcome him to the house forgetting their pride or ego. This is a good start of an important relationship.

In old days the marriageable couple and their families were new to each other, and such a tradition made utmost sense. Today marriages require prior approvals, verifications and confirmations. Yet the parents' worries and concerns regarding their daughter's welfare in their husband's house remain the same, which makes the ritual relevant to this day.

33. Why is there a dress code for sacred rituals and mar-riages?

There are two types of dress codes for Hindus. At the time of performing holy rituals, people are advised to wear loose and comfortable clothes. As we are required to sit for a long time in the same position during such rituals, we need be comfortable first if we are to be able to concentrate on the shlokas and mantras.

There is a different dress code for weddings. The bride and the groom dress like a king and a queen.

Let me tell you an interesting story. In the old days, even if a king passing through the road would have to give way to the groom. As the groom is at the most critical turning point of his life, he is treated as no less than the king for the day. Today his challenges begin. From one to two. Establishing the household, and preparing for the children, their studies and upbringing and so on. At this turning point of one's life, everyone's good wishes and encouragement become vital.

34. Why do we offer an odd amount like 11, 51, 101 to our near and dear ones on special occasions or sacred ceremonies?

Let us consider this question from the lens of social science. When we want to recognize someone's valuable contribution or work, we reward or award him/her to convey our best wishes.   Hindus don't award an even amount as a reward money, but add a coin to make the sum an odd number.

There is no mention of such a rule in any Hindu scripture. The custom developed over the years to help communicate our pleasure and support for a person's achievement. This also helps the person raise money to meet the expenses incurred during the process or work.
dt

When we give a hundred rupee note with one addition coin, we are reminding the person that in order to make it 200,- the calculation must start from 1. We are giving an extra piece to nudge the person to achieve more. Now it is the recipient's duty to go to the next level and double the sum. e This is also related to a common saying, "99 ka chakkar." The person, who accepts the sum of 101, gets trapped into putting more efforts to make it 200 or more.

35. Fish is used for decoration in east Indian marriages. Why?

In the eastern parts of India, Bengal, fish plays a very important role in one's life. It's part of the daily diet, and considered almost vegetarian. To some this may come as a surprise. Fish is considered to be a non-vegetarian food everywhere. The local surroundings, regional practices and conditions influence all religions. In the coastal area where fish is easily available compared to green vegetables, people adopted their food habits long before the religion was adopted by them. This hasn't changed even today. In Bengal, a Brahmin can eat fish as food has direct relation to his life, and his religion and spirituality has direct relation to his soul.

Decorating with fish allows people to see the skill of the housewife in making the food attractive and also to mark respect to the most commonly food in the region.

36. Why do Hindus put tilak on their forehead? Why do married Hindu women put tilak and sindoor on the parting on their forehead?

The place between eyebrows on the forehead where Hindus put tilak is called the gyan bindu — the center of knowledge. The vein which provides seeing, smelling, tasting and hearing inputs to brain passes through it. The tilak helps us restrict, regulate and filter stimulus by slowing down our reflexes. What we see, hear, taste or smell has to be understood and evaluated carefully before we jump to any conclusion. If the information passing to the brain is balanced and controlled, we'll allow the Vivek (reason or intellect) to rise and prevail in us, and it'd help us react wisely.

Secondly, we pay our respect to intellectuals and scholars by putting a tilak on their forehead. The tilak is a mark of our recognition and appreciation of their knowledge and contribution to the society.

37. Why do Hindu women feel the need to cover their face with ghoonghat?

Ghoonghat wasn't originally a Hindu custom. Our gods and goddesses eweren't depicted with covered faces. There is no mention of such a tradition in any Hindu scriptures. usThis custom seeped into our culture during Mughal rule. When the Mughals ruled major parts of Indian subcontinent, it was adopted as customary in place of a burqa.

In Islam, women wear burqa to cover their body and the face with a veil. During the Muslim rule, Hindus were forced to adopt the custom, especially in northern, north central parts of India, Haryana and Rajasthan. However, it's not prevalent in South India, where sMuslims didn't have much influence.

It is fascinating to see how religions and customs are influenced by politics and confusions and misrepresentations arise over time. It helps to keep an open and curious mind when it comes to religious beliefs and practices.

38. Why is the Hindu husband called Pati Parmeshwar? Shouldn't there be a day or custom to worship wives?

Historically the division of work between men and women depended on their physical conditions. A male body is comparably healthy and strong, whereas a female experiences fatigue and weakness during period and pregnancy. When the two start a family, the labor-intensive work was the responsibility of the man, and the light work the domain of the woman.

The husband goes out to hunt, fish or farm, while the wife cooks the food, cleans and looks after their home. As the man had the responsibility to go out in the outside world where there were enough predators and competition, he had to be well-prepared, fit and strong. This allowed him to become the head of the family. As he provided for his family and took care of their well-being, he was called Pati Parmeswar, the god of the home.

Now the time and living standards have changed. There are opportunities for both men and women. Yet the family tradition that gives protection and strength, and a special status to men remains. If one says that the man represents the mind in the family and the woman represent its heart, it wouldn't be wrong. The care, concern and respect given to and from both husband and wife to each other will make their marital life happier and perfect.

Death

39. What is the difference between a burial and a cremation?

To cremate or to bury sa dead body depends on more than the religious practice, and also on the place, time and available facilities to treat the body. In the Indian subcontinent, there was no shortage of wood, thus cremation was a reasonable way to dispose bodies. The birth of Islam happened in a desert where wood wasn't readily available, and the only option was to bury the dead. Christianity comes from Europe, where snow covers the land almost half the year. Burying was their natural choice.

Cremation seems a cleaner and quicker method to treat a dead body. One didn't know the actual cause of death in ancient times so fire was a safe bet to kill germs and prevent infectious diseases. Fire helped mitigate the spread of diseases. Today modern crematoriums provide the same facility in forms of incinerators l.

,d

40. Why is Sutak observed during birth as well as death in the Hindu family?

After giving birth, the mother needs complete bed rest to regain her strength. She keeps discharging fluid and odor for some time even after birth, and both mother and family members risk infection. Based on the role a person plays in society, the days of sutak are defined. For a Brahmin, it is for ten days, twelve days for Kshatriya, sixteen for Vaisya and for Shudra thirty days. The longest time is advised for Shudra as they do the most physical work. Nowadays birth deliveries take place in hospitals, and there is proper medicine to treat and manage infection so things have changed, which wasn't the case before.

Similarly, Sutak is observed at the time of death in the family. This is common for 13 days for all. On the 13th day the community comes together for a ritual and then return to their daily lives. This has scientific as well as social reasons: Sutak safeguards the person and the family at large by ensuring no communicable diseases or infections spread from the dead to the living.

One did not always know the reason of death in old days. Anything could lead to one's death — sickness, prolonged diseases, old age, etc. People from the family involved in taking care of the sick or the old person may carry the infection/disease elsewhere. So they stay within the boundaries of their house. After cleaning and bathing for few days, it is hoped that they are free of all infection and safe to go out.   nenSutak also allows the family members to remember the departed for few days, cherish their memories and then life has to go on.

Today Sutak has almost been almost ignored. We should be more careful to maintain cleanliness and hygiene.

41. What is Shraddh? Why do we offer food to the needy on this day?

Shraddh Paksh is observed during Bhadrapad Mah, which falls in the month of September when monsoon is near its end. The earth is wet and the Sun shines intensely after many days of overcast skies. Imagine the effect of having two life giving elements at its peak – sun (heat) and moisture (water). This is the time when fertility is on its peak in animals and plants.

D uring this month all Hindus go to serve food to needy people and earn Punya in the name of our ancestors who have died. To offer our love and best wishes for rebirth in a right yoni or form. This is out of love for the departed. In which yoni, the departed will take rebirth ultimately depends on their own karma or actions in their earlier birth. But the present generation offer Punya for them out of love.

During this period, we offer sweet milk and rice (khir) to crows — they are considered as ambassador to our ancestors. There is interesting story attached to this ritual. The crows eat what you offer them. From their waste, plants like Pipal can grow. The Pipal has no seedst —- it grows from the crows' waste . This tree has a long life and considered precious to Lord Vishnu. The food and sweet offered to the crows indirectly help plant and grow these large oxygen-giving trees.

42. What is the reason of performing rituals on 3rd, 10th and 13th day after the death?

It is believed that the soul of the deceased remains around living family members for three days. The soul isn't ready to accept the loss of the body after death. Slowly after three days, it realizes the fact of losing the body. As mentioned in Garuda Puran, the book on death and rebirth, these rituals help the soul merge with the universe, and prepare them to return in a new avatar or birth. And the family members must pray for the soul to take a peaceful departure from the home of the earlier birth.

If we look at the scientific aspect of the rituals, we can say that when a person is dead, he or she leaves many people behind, who may love, respect and depend on the departed. They remember and pay their respect to the dead, and are grateful for their presence in their lives, and now the time has come to say goodbye and pray for his or her soul to rest in peace. This is one way to come back to normal life after such a loss and bereavement.

III. Worship, Rituals & Festivities

Worship

43. 'Om' is used frequently in Hindu rituals. What is its meaning and significance?

'Om' is the sound of the universe. In the Santana Dharma, this is called the biz mantra. No word is as perfect as Om. The easiest route to enter a full meditative state is its correct pronunciation or chanting. The sound is first generated from the stomach; it gradually rises to the heart and the throat, and discharged through the scalp. The sound-vibration of Om helps attain peace internally within our bodies.

No mantra is complete without Om — which opens a clear communication channel with the God. There have been thorough studies on how the sound of Om encompasses every sound of every language known to mankind. But I would say Om is more than a sound, it's the vibration of the universe – all coming from within us making us one with the universe. Perhaps that explains the meditative qualities of Om.

44. Why do we blow Shankh during poojas?

There are three reasons for blowing shankh during poo-jas. This is the first tool discovered by our ancestors to create effective sound. One can say it was the first musical instrument created by nature. When you blow a shankh, you create a loud sound which informs the people around the temple that a poo-ja is being performed. They may either come to join you or pray from their respective place at that point of time.

The most plausible reason for blowing shankh is to create a sound in the house to dispel unwanted objects or insects from the house. Research shows the ultrasonic component of the sound works effectively on humans, birds, insects and mi-crobes as well.

Blowing shankh is also a very good exercise for lungs.

45. Why is the worship of Lord Ganesh performed first in Hindu rituals and pooja everywhere?

ee sIn the world of management, there is tool known as PDCA (Plan, Do, Check, Act or Adjust), where planning comes first. A good beginning is a work half done! Lord Ganesh is the symbol of knowledge and intelligence. By worshiping Ganesh ji first, we make a mental note to complete all necessary preparations or planning before we embark on a new day, project or business. Whether in business or life, it's always a good idea to plan carefully before starting a new journey. Worshipping Ganesh ji first teaches us the secret to success in all our endeavors: careful deliberation and planning.
t

Lord Ganesh is represented with a head of an elephant, which has the biggest brain and strongest memory. By worshiping Ganesh ji, we are paying an indirect respect to all the knowledgeable and intelligent creatures in the universe. With our prayers, we are indirectly reminding ourselves to seek and take into consideration advice and consent from elders and experts in the field.

While praying to Lord Ganesh, we indirectly tell ourselves that the mission has now begun. Let's go ahead and make sure we are ready — everything is ready. Later during the pooja, nothing should come in our way to stop us from completing it. The same holds true in our daily lives. Any work started without careful planning do not end happily. The desired outcome is guaranteed only if all the necessary preparations are completed before embarking upon the task or mission. Praying to Lord Ganesh is a call for the use of brain, and it is Lord Ganesh who give us the intelligence and knowhow to tackle a difficult task or mission successfully.t

46. What is the significance and science behind the tradition of Yagna?

Yagna is a Vedic sacrifice found in Yajurveda, and practiced for devotion through fire worship. Fire is a powerful force of nature, and considered to be a living embodiment of God.   We offer our gratitude to all Gods by way of offering our most lovable, important possessions (at least in old times), grains. Yagna is performed with mantras and shlokas chants in front of the fire either by individuals or groups in presence of a qualified priest.

These are some important facts about Yagna:

- The fire kills and clears unwanted bacteria from the environment.
- The cow dung, ghee, wood and grains sprinkled in the fire create a special aroma which makes people feel good and happy.
- The unique combination of heat, aroma, sound of Vedic mantras and special occasion help create the right mood and peaceful environment for everyone.
- Before we create this mood, we summon our gods and ancestors to pay our respect and take their blessings. It's a unique Hindu tradition to keep us connected with our roots.
- The smoke from the sacred fire moistens and cleans our eyes. The heat glows our skin, and helps with nasal congestion. This smoke is very different from the pollution we face in the streets outside our homes today.

According to a Russian scientist, the cow milk can protect us from atomic radiation; cow dung has anti-radiation quality as well. According to the research, when the ghee derived from cows is sprinkled in Yagna fire, its fumes lessen the effects of atomic radiation to a great extent.

The Yagna as per microbiology is also lethal for acaroid in

nature. One has to be amazed by the amount of knowledge and insight our Rishi-munies had on such matters.

47. Why do we worship inside a temple? Why do we have to visit the temple to perform a pooja?

Temples and churches are places of religious congregation where all sections of a society can come together to receive preaching from priests and scholars. Not everyone has a prayer room in their house where they can concentrate and meditate peacefully. Temples allow people to come together, perform rituals, and return home with a renewed faith, good learnings and sweet prasad. The religious beliefs are transmitted to masses through these public sermons and gatherings. By constructing temples, we also help expand our religion and its teachings, and help improve the quality of people's personal and social lives i.e. Jana Kalyan.

The site for the construction of a temple is chosen after carefully studying the geography, and the general vibe of the location and the environment. The site must be peaceful, and closer to nature to provide an escape from day-to-day worldly distractions. The temple is constructed as per traditional architectural plan and design. Almost all religious monuments adhere to a sturdy pyramid-like design, which helps create the feeling of being closer to our inner strength —soul, god— and the nature.

48. Why do Hindus use the right hand to perform poojas?

Our brain has two parts: left and right. The left brain controls the right hand and the right brain controls the left hand. Our left brain is a long-term storage, responsible for deep memories, which define our core personality and character. The right brain controls short-term activities. In the computer language we can say our right brain is the desktop and the left brain our CPU.

Any work done by the right hand goes to the left brain, and the same shapes our core. That's why our gurus insist upon using the right hand while performing poojas and holy rituals for long-term impact and benefit.

49. Why aren't shoes allowed inside Hindu temples?

t   Shoes save our feet from mud and dirt, sharp objects, creatures and impurities on the road, and from extreme cold or excessive heat. When you enter a temple with shoes, you are entering with all these undesirable things and impurities in the temple. This disturbs the clean and meditative environment inside the temple.

The Hindu religion grew in India where wearing shoes throughout the year didn't make sense as it did in the western world climates where lack of shoes can be deadly. In India, you could in fact relax your feet by walking with bare feet on the ground a good part of the year. You'll also notice that temples usually have marble or stone floor that relaxes bare feet. Wearing shoes on such a ground is actually counterproductive.

Rituals are tools that help achieve desired results of the religion. And these rituals reflect environment and times of when they were first created.

50. Why do Hindus chant mantras?

The universe is full of natural vibrations or rhythm which have effects on every living creature, be it human, insects or plans. In the army, if solders are marching in a parade and comes across a bridge, they stop marching and walk across the bridge. They are careful enough to prevent manmade vibrations from interfering with the natural vibrations that may cause the bridge to collapse. Likewise, we know how useful ultrasound can be for various medical procedures. In modern medical science, it is used for investigations, identification as well as for treatment.

The Gayatri mantra and its vibrations have been investigated and analyzed by scientists worldwide. And it has been concluded that it is one of the most powerful vibrations for cleaning the environment and treatment of disease. By chanting a specific mantra, we generate vibrations within our body as well as the environment. This makes the desirable changes within and around us. When we chant, the vibrations created by the sound and breath meddles with the natural vibrations of nature and creates a specific effect.

There are thousands of mantras in our Vedas and Upanishad for various purposes and different occasions. They are designed according to one's requirements, needs and treatment.

51. Grass and tree leaves are offered to the god during poojas. Why?

This ritual has been in practice for centuries. In old days, there were no or very small houses to protect people from extreme conditions. People spent most of their time out in the open, and poojas were performed on open grounds under the sky, closer to the nature. Over a period of time, the houses got bigger, and poojas could now be performed indoors. Grass is offered to the god as per the old tradition to bring the feeling of the nature and farm inside the house.

Similarly, there used to be limited utensils in the house. Large plant leaves like banana and mango were used in place of plates and utensils those days. Banana leaves were also used to cover the deity's statue. wNow they are placed inside the house to make the god feel that he is in the open farm and closer to the nature.

In Satya Narayan Pooja, we cover the statue with banana leaves. We place mango leaves on the main door of our house. This shows our respect for nature. We say that Lord Krishna lives in the Pipal leaf. That is because the leaf is sort of a square and we can put some Prasad to offer him, hence the saying. The darbha is lovely for Lord Ganesh as the ganapati idol is made out of mud, and the mud and darbha grow together.

In short, there was a necessity to use these natural items during poojas earlier, but now it is merely symbolic.

52. Why is the Pipal tree worshiped by Hindus?

The Pipal tree or sacred fig (*Ficus Religiosa*) is from the family of Moraceae — one of the giant trees which discharges oxygen at night. It's incredible how the ancient Rishis-Munis could possess such botanical insight then. Today all over the world people are talking about climate change and the need to save our environment. The air is polluted due to many contaminations: chemicals, gases and smoke. Inhaling polluted air pose risks to our health. It is time to reconcile the insight and practice of the old rishis and munis to save earth. They identified and mastered the roots of environmental equilibrium, which is a matter of great inspiration for all. They set down rules and rituals to help protect the nature and the environment.

In *Gita*, Lord Krishna says, "I am Pipal as it is." The life-giving Pipal tree is divine, and gives maximum pran vayu (oxygen) to the mankind. According to Buddhist lores, Lord Buddha meditated and gained enlightenment under a sacred fig called the Bodhi tree. Through the worship of the Pipal tree, we can bring environmental awareness in the society. Religion can move beyond the boundaries of spirituality. In other words, spirituality is not independent of the quality of life. All that is required to make the life more meaningful has been brought under the umbrella of religion. This is the beauty of Hindu religion.

53. During a pooja, why do we invoke all gods and our ancestors in the beginning and end?

Let me tell you a simple truth: Life is worship. Our daily routine, our day to day activities are all centered around oneself. Every human act is based on the fundamental need to improve, maintain or manage available resources to sustain or improve life on Earth.

We perform pooja for two reasons: to celebrate life, and to improve it. By invoking all Gods and our ancestors, we create a conducive environment to concentrate and detach ourselves from the disillusionment of our mind and surroundings. Every God in Hindu religion has a different role or representation: Ganesh stands for intelligence, Vishnu for management, Shiva for peace and eliminating bad evils, Nav-Graha Devta for management of environment, etc. We invoke our ancestors to acknowledge their contribution in our life, and our origins. It is a celebration and recognition of our predecessors' contribution to one's life and wellbeing.

In Hindu philosophy, an individual is never alone. You are together with your family and the world. Your small victories and defeats, the little joys and big sorrows, are also that of your family.

54. How are Jain and Buddhism different from Hindu religion?

Jain and Hindu religions are part of Sanatan Dharma. They are not different religions. In my opinion all who believe in the following principles are Hindus:

1. Those who believe in birth after the death (re-birth)
2. Those who believe in the principle of Karma.
3. Those who believe in the philosophy of peace or nirvana as the ultimate aim of life.

With the above beliefs, both Buddhism and Jainism are part of Sanatan Dharma.

55. What is ISKCON? Is it possible to get Darshanam of God?

International Society for Krishna Consciousness (ISKCON) is a Bhakti-based religious organization formed by Swamy Prabhupada in 1966 in New York, USA. He was a Vedic spiritual leader, who believed that a common man can reach the God through Bhakti Marg or the path of worship. If one should surrender to Lord Krishna and believe in the principles of holiness, he can feel the presence of God around.

In the Hindu religion, there are multiple ways to reach the God. These are three ways, in particular:

1. Bhakti (Worship): This is the simplest form of reaching the God. This calls for devotion by heart and mind. Once you do this, you feel ego is gone, and you are near to God.
2. Dhyan (Meditation): This is another way to attain the ultimate peace; you will be nearer to God.
3. Shodh (Research): This is an approach adopted by ancient Rishis-Munis based on close reading of discourses in Vedas and Upanishads.

In the case of ISKCON, Swamy Prabhupada suggested Bhakti as one of the ways to be nearer to God. This form of worship or meditation has produced results for devotees.

56. What is the place of Bhakti Marg in Hindu philosophy?

The Hindu religion has a unique approach to be closer to God. Bhakti Marg is for the common people. In most religions, there are common rules and guidelines for everyone to follow. In Hindu religion, there are multiple methods suggested to reach God. If you want to devote your whole life to Dharma, you may adopt Shodh Marg. You may study the Vedas and Upanishads and attain the ultimate God, which may be time-consuming, and one may have to devote their whole life for it. The Bhakti Marg is much flexible — you can devote any time you have to recite bhajans and mantras toward the attainment of God or a satisfied life.

57. What is the relationship between Hare Krishna and Aghoris sadhus?

These are two different philosophies. Ramanujan was a scholar who believed in Bhakti Marg to attain Lord Vishnu and his Avatars. Total devotion to Vishnu will be the only way to attain Moksha. Ramanujan believed that Vedas and Upanishad will give knowledge but if one wants to reach the God, this knowledge is not sufficient. One must follow the path of Bhakti and devotion to reach the Lord.

The Aghoris is a different line of philosophy; they believe devotion can touch the soul and merge with brahma. They are primarily attached to Lord Shiva and his contacts — Brahma and soul. The devotees need grit to have contact with God and talk one to one. This is one type of Hatha yoga, where you need a strong desire and zeal to be with God. The devotee goes to extreme stage to feel near to God, and he wants to remain in that state for a long time.

58. Why is Rajneesh such a controversial figure? How do we attain complete bliss?

Acharya Rajneesh's philosophy is nearer to Astavakra Geeta. He criticized the implementation of the Hindu Dharma in our societies. It is necessary to adapt, correct or eliminate religious laws as times and societies change. Some of his radical ideas include free love, free sex, and their children to be handed over to the government for care. These revolutionary ideas are not part of the Hindu religion. These ideas may be okay for the developed world, but are not quite suitable for India and Hindu religion. This made his teachings controversial.

I still feel, barring a few of his speeches and illustration, in general, he is uniquely extraordinary. He questioned many set rules of our society, and he is thus valuable. His method of meditation is very good for a common man, and worth adopting. He also focused on Dhyan, the meditation.

59. Who are Vaishnavs? Is wealth and prosperity necessary to attain God or moksha?

The Vaishnav sect is a part of Hindu religion. They worship Lord Vishnu and his avatars. The Vaishnavs have many branches, like Ramanujam, who believe in Tyag and complete devotion to Lord Krishna. The Swami Narayan sect worship Lord Krishna. The Swami Narayan sect and the Pustimargiya sect are both family-oriented with large numbers of devotees.

The Vaishnavs believe that a man should continue to do karma (action) with all devotion based on set guidelines and a part of his profit must be contributed to the sects. This is how they serve the society and take care of the needy people. The idea is simple: you cannot serve the society unless you are capable to give. You can only give when you have something in surplus. This is one way to serve God. Pusti Marg is a path to reach God through fulfilment.

Service to society is also a way to reach the God.

60. The faces and dresses of the same god varies from temple to temple. Which is the right one, if the God is same?

No common man has ever seen a god. Anyone who claims so cannot picture the god in a particular face or dress. We believe through literature that the god is everywhere, in every particle and atom of this world. At the same time it is also said that the god lives in everyone's heart. Those who deeply meditate form a particular image of the god in their mind and heart. They see the god through their own points of references: ethnicity, culture and understanding of the world. The preachers and seekers build idols to explain their conception of the god according to the culture of their people.

The many faces of the gods and goddesses represent the sculptor or their patron's values and beliefs depending on the stories of the particular area, people and even themselves. What's important is not the face or the dress but your own faith and understanding of an idol. The physical representation of the god makes you feel as if you're in his presence in the prayer room or temple. This is one way of worshiping and getting closer to the divine power. However this is not enough. We have to practice the religious teachings in our own life: serve the poor and better the society through right action and meaningful contribution. This is the only way we can truly reach god.

It is not wise to visit temple, pay superficial respect and expect all kinds of favors from the god. Let us not define the relationship with the god as that of a supplier and a customer. We pay donation to the temple and expect multiplication from the god. We forget that he is not your supplier, and you are not his customer.

Rituals & Festivities

61. What are the rituals for a person from birth till death?

The Hindu rituals are accurately designed from conception to birth and death. Here I would like to mention sixteen Sanskars that span an individual's lifetime.

1. Garbha-Dharan Sanskar: This is a Sanskar to decide the time, period and plan for conceiving a pregnancy. It is rarely observed these days. In the past, pregnancy used to be planned according to Muhurt to give birth to a child during the most healthy and favorable condition, both inside and outside the house.

2. Punsavana Sanskar: Upon pregnancy, the elders in the family blessed the woman and her child with shlokas for good mental and physical development in the mother's womb. Today we visit the doctor to get the mother examined for the same.

3. Simanta Sanskar: This is performed on the eighth month of pregnancy to receive blessings from the elders and family members. If it's a first pregnancy, the mother is taken to her parents' house. The first delivery is supposed to take place at the mother's house to ensure her ease, comfort and well-being.

4. Jaat Karma Sanskar: This is performed after the child is born. There are mantras and shlokas to give blessings for a long and healthy life.

5. Namkaran Sanskar: When the child is 11 days old, the name is disclosed to the society with advice from family astrologer. Normally the first letter of the name is decided on the basis of presence of the moon in the child's kundali. The moon's presence reflects the mental temperament of the child. A set of letters are attached to all the rashis, and accordingly the name is decided. Of course, it is not essential for all.

6. Nishkraman Sanskar: This Sanskar is normally performed after four months of birth to pray for good health and positive mental attitude of the child. Mantras and shlokas are recited to create a positive environment in the house. By this time the child is free from memories of the last janma or birth, and can start observing the present birth and environment.

7. Anna Prashan Sanskar: This is performed six months after birth. The tooth starts growing, and solid food is finally offered to the child. The mother is taught what and how to offer food to the child by the elders in the family.

8. Mundan Sanskar: This ritual is performed when thet child reaches the age of three, and his head is shaved for the first time. This is very important to observe to get rid of the hair grown from the time of birth. The scalp of the child is very soft and the use of any sharp-edged tool to shave the head could be dangerous. The senior and experienced members are called to witness and aid.

9.

10. Vidya Arambh Sanskar: This Sanskar introduces the child to all items required for acquiring education: books, notebooks, pens, pencils and inkpot. The child is helped to write the first letter "OM" on the paper by hand.

11. Karna Vedan Sanskar: Ears are punched during this ritual to sharpen the mind and for ornaments. There is a belief that the vein which goes to brain from ear boosts intelligence if punctured properly.

12. Upnayan or Ygnopavitt Sanskar: This Sanskar is very important. The child is now ready to go to ashram to acquire knowledge with blessings from the family for a bright and right future. The child goes to ashram (hostel) to gain education and expertise in areas of his interest under the guid-

ance of Guru.

13. Vedarambha Sanskar: This is to start one's education of Vedas and Upanishads. In the Hindu religious education system, the suitability to acquire knowledge is judged before giving the knowledge. A teacher assesses the person through their character and temperament, and only then decides to accept him or her as a pupil.

14. Keshant Sanskar: After completing of Gurukul education, the pupil shaves his head. When he entered the Ashram, he came with a shaved head. Now he is leaving ashram as a responsible and knowledgeable person to serve the society.

15. Samavartan Sanskar: aAfter completing the education, the pupil returns home. The society welcomes him back to his home, and he is now seen as a responsible person. On performing this Sanskar, the rest of the people know that the person is back and can now be given work or responsibility. The king knows and this is like waiting for an offer of a job or work. This Sanskar now opens door for marriage proposals. End of Brahmcharya.

16. Vivah Sanskar: Marriage is also a Sanskar. The person marries as per Vedic tradition. In the presence of Agni, a sacred oath is taken by both husband and wife to understand and support each other. With shlokas and rituals, the couple is directed to commit to a respectable life, and show care, concern and respect for each other. They now begin the Grihasth ashram.

17. Antyesti Sanskar: One should also know the art of dying. Before death one has many responsibilities to complete. In the Hindu religion, death is not end of life but a beginning of yet another life hereafter. This Sanskar is a fixed ritual for thirteen days to be performed by the family after the death.

Hinduism is perhaps the only religion in the world   that

turns an individual into an asset for the society through a series
of Sanskars or rituals to mark important stages of one's life.
The Hindu child is educated and oriented to be a responsible
citizen dedicated to the family and the society. If such a
process is adopted in every religion, there will be peace and
prosperity everywhere. This is the main objective of Sanatan
Dharma.

62. What are the major festivals of Hindu religion?

These are four major festivals in Hinduism: Diwali, Holi, Raksha Bandhan and Dashahra.

1. **Diwali:** Diwalii is the biggest festival of Hindus. It is the festival of lights celebrated after the rainy season is over. The crops are ready and now people wait for harvest. By this time, they know the likely size of the yield. To the business classes earlier based on crops, the financial year comes to an end on this day. Profit is calculated and celebrated.

There is another event linked to Diwali. After killing Ravana in Lanka, Lord Rama returns to Ayodhya and to celebrate the return of their king after 14 long years, people decorate the whole city with lights. Since then the practice of cleaning the house and painting started, a healthy measure after four long months of rains.

This is primarily a festival for Vaishya, the business classes.

2. **Holi:** Holi is the festival of colors after the winter crops have been planted, and farmers and farm laborers are free to celebrate.

According to the story behind the festival, King Hiranykashayp attempted to get his own son Prahalad killed because he worshiped Lord Vishnu, who had killed his brother in fight. His sister, Holika, proposes to kill Prahlad by entering a burning pyre with Prahlad. She says that will not be affected by fire but Prahlad will be burnt alive. The situation changes when Vayu Devta blows away Holika's fireproof blanket, and Prahalad is saved by Lord Vishnu. Holika burns to death instead. Moral of the story: one should have faith in God. He will come to the rescue of his bhaktas and save them from any harm or evil.

This festival is primarily for working classes.

3. Raksha Bandhan: This festival celebrates the love of sister and brother. The sister ties a thread of raksha on the wrist of her brother and prays for a long and healthy life for him. In return, the brother promises to provide her safety and security.

This is also a festival for Brahmin to perform special Puja of Rudri reciting and change of Ygnopavitt (Janeu). The Brahmins also tie a thread on the wrist of their followers. This is supposed to be the biggest festival for all the Brahmins.

4. Dashahra: This festival comes 20 days before Diwali. This is the day when the Ravana was killed by Lord Rama. This is a celebration of the victory of good over evil. All arms and weapons are cleaned and worshipped during the festival.

This is supposed to be the biggest festival for all the Kshatriyas: kings and administrators.

63. What are the four dhams?

About 2000 years ago, Adi Shankaracharya the Hindu scholar and priest formed four maths. Every Hindu is expected to visit these places once in a lifetime to attain Moksha. The four maths are:

1. Badrinath: Situated in North India, this is a temple where Lord Vishnu performed Tapasya (meditation) for many years. And to protect him from extreme cold, Laxmi took the avatar of a plant and covered him. This is a Nar-Narayan swaroop of Vishnu. It represents a grihasth (family) avatar, and people visit the temple to seek blessings for a successful family life.

2. Rameshwaram: This Shiva temple in South India is said to have been built by Lord Rama before going to Lanka to fight Ravana. If you are going to war, it better be for a just cause supported and blessed by the supreme power. Lord Rama, the avatar of Vishnu, is praying for blessing and approval from Lord Shiva, the god of destruction. Before restarting to himsa (violence), you must think a thousand times, and ensure that you have the blessings and approval of the higher or proper authority.

3. Dwarika: It is a temple of Lord Krishna in West India. After completing his childhood Leela in Mathura and Vrindavan, he took part in the Pandava-Kaurava war to protect dharma. After the war, he came to Dwarika to spend his rest of the life, and attain moksha. No matter how big you are, the end is same for everyone i.e. death with or without moksha.

4. Jagannath Puri: In East India, there is an idol of Lord Krishna with his brother Balram and sister Subhadra on the same platform. In Kalyug, Jagannath is seen as Vishnu, Balram as Mahesh and Subhadra as Brahma. Today love and respect for each other in the family is important in our individualistic

society where family bonding is not valued. One should learn to respect one's own family, its role and values. The family is the first school of sanskars.

The purpose of visiting these four dhams once in a life-time benefits the pilgrims in many ways. They get the opportunity to see the whole country and learn about different places and cultures. Normally old people after their retirement or when they have spare money, they go for such yatras. When they return home, they are now able to introduce the younger lot in their family and circle to the rich stories and diverse thoughts linked to these places. This gives good Sanskar to the young.

64. In every ritual, the priest recites Sanskrit shlokas. Why cannot they use contemporary language for the same?

The religious shlokas written as poetry come from the Vedas and Upanishads written in Sanskrit. They contain a pre-defined instruction for carrying out a puja in a particular method. Written by ancient scholars as poetry and lyric, and composed in a musical way, they create a good and positive feeling in people's hearts and minds.

In the past Sanskrit was largely understood by the common man, and it was not necessary for a priest to translate. Nowadays people have no time or interest in translation. Thus it has become a mechanical custom. Even if some priests desire to translate, we have no patience to listen to them. The focus has now shifted toward dance and dhamal on such occasions.

The Sanskrit shloks are easily some of the most beautiful and musical lyrics in any language. We must insist for their translation in our languages. We must ask our priest to explain the meaning behind each shloka so that we understand the significance of the ritual and practice. Every shloka contains very important message for the good of the society. Translation could be one of the ways to renew interest among the younger generation about our religion, and build respect for it.

65. Why do we wear new clothes on Diwali? Why do we use crackers and lighting?

Diwali is the last day of the Hindu Year. A day to tally profit and loss, and prepare the annual balance sheet for businessmen. Following which they take a break, enjoy vacation and gear up for the next year's challenge. The new clothes reflects our success and readiness to welcome the new year. All old ledgers are closed, and new books of accounts are opened. We take our books for pooja to receive blessings of guru and elders.

There is one more reason to buy new clothes. Diwali is usually celebrated in the month of October or November. This period marks the start of winter. Diwali clothes help prepare for cold weather as well.

Here it is important to note monsoon precedes Diwali. The end of monsoon with humidity and heat in the air is breeding ground for bacteria and germs that could spread diseases like malaria, dengue and viral fever. We get a chance to clean and remove unwanted stuff from the house during Diwali to prevent probable causes of infections. Firecrackers kill unwanted bacteria and germs through heat and smoke. However, these days firecrackers cause more harm than good due to overuse, population growth, noise and air pollution.

)d.

66. What is Panchamrut? What is its importance?

Panchamrut has both religious importance and practical value in everyone's life. tIt contains five (panch) amrut i.e. nectars of god: milk, curd, honey, ghee, and sugar. This mixture is used to cleanse idols and offered as prasad to god and later distributed in small quantity to all disciples.

Each of these five ingredients help our skin glow. Curd is a natural cleanser, and milk a natural moisturizer. Honey is an antibiotic, while ghee is a lubricant, and sugar or misri a scrubber. This unique potion is good for both internal and external use. It is also a remedy for minor stomach upsets and intestinal issues.

67. What is the meaning of Sathiya, and why is the symbol painted everywhere during religious rituals?

In Hindu religion, Sathiya symbolizes gati (speed) and power. It has four blades with edges that bend clockwise. It represents movement, and movement with speed generates power. In a way this represents the movement of time, and generation of life. Life, time, power, thoughts and actions — they all have a moving quality and that is the way of the universe. When we feel the need for a change, we enter a new phase of growth and development in our lives. Sathiya symbolizes our acceptance for the need for the change, from present to past, and from past to future.
r

68. On the day of Shitla-Satam, why do we eat food cooked the previous day?

Shitla-Satam falls on the day before Janmastami, when monsoon is at its peak. In Hindu religion, we do not fire the oven (chulha) on this day. On this day, the women in the house take rest from their daily chore (cooking), and we normally eat food cooked the previous day.

This festival comes during the peak of rainy season. During monsoon, our body and digestive system is vulnerable to diseases. By eating a day-old food, we are preparing our stomach to digest old and cold food; we are making it work a bit harder. Digestion may take a little longer. So on the next day, the day of Janmasatami, we fast. This process disrupts the digestive system and makes it more efficient and agile. On the day of Shitla-Saptami, we also eat Rayta (a dish made out of mustard seed and curd) with the stale food to fire up our digestive system.

69. What is Satya Narayan Katha?

Satya Narayan Katha is a very popular Hindu tradition. It probably started as a process of explaining and interpreting the Hindu laws and practices to the people. Probably it was the time when rules were first made to govern the society. As there were no rulers at the time, Hindu saints and philosophers were recognized as the representatives of god and their word became the law. Stories and examples were devised to help explain these laws to the commoners.

The Satya Narayan Katha consists of stories for all four classes of the society. There is story of a Brahmin who decides to worship Lord Vishnu, and perform the Katha, and gets his dream fulfilled. There is a second story about a hard-working laborer, a woodcutter, who decides to worship Lord Vishnu and also gets his dream fulfilled. The third story is of a Kshatriya (a king) who decides to worship the lord, but only upon leaving his ego, his purpose get fulfilled. But the story of a Vaishya (a baniya), the business class, goes on for a long time, as he lies and doesn't keep his promises. Finally when he realizes his sin, his dream also gets fulfilled.

All the stories have the following conclusions:

- Have faith in God. Believe in truth. Never lie.
- Doing good in this birth will decide your next birth.
- If the promise is made, fulfill it. Value your commitment.
- Good and bad will have consequences in the same birth.

By collectively listening to this Katha, according to the tradition, we understand the basic principles of a peaceful life. This is Punya. The Katha is a very simple and effective tool to teach the society moral and ethical principles for life.

70. Why is Shasthi-Poorty?

Shasthi-Poorty is the remarriage of an old couple arranged by their children once their parents reach the age of 60. It is between the same couple, of course. 60 is the age of retirement as well. Ideally the man who has prepared the next generation to take over his family legacy is a happy onesd. All children arrange a puja together, and invite their near and dear ones to the occasion. They celebrate their parents' remarriage, which is something that once happened before their birth.

Now the old couple feel free from all household responsibilities. They can begin to enjoy a balanced life with intense togetherness, move around and fulfill their remaining dreams, which were not possible while leading a busy family life.

71. What is Sahastra Chandra Darshanam?

Sahastra Chandra Darshanam is celebrated for a man who is alive and has seen 1000 full moon days in his life. This comes somewhere between 81 or 82 years of one's age. On this day, children, relatives, near and dear ones assemble and perform a puja. Water from Holy Rivers is poured upon the old man from a sieve of 1000 holes to give him a bath. All the children take the water collected from his body and keep it in the house. The old man thereafter is considered equal to God.

This is a very wonderful and unique ritual which recognizes the value of an old man in the house. Normally person at this age is ignored and considered as commodity and kept in one corner of the house or kept in an old age home. Such a function make the person recognize his contribution to the family and to the society. This brings joy in one's life and creates a sense of accomplishment. It is also a message to the old man that now he is at the level of God and must play the role of a spectator and give advice only when he is asked for it. People visit their temples and pray to the God, and only then He blesses them.

72. What is the purpose of Dhundh on Holi? Why is the newborn child taken near the fire for blessings?

Holi marks the completion of winter. The Holi fire is a holy fire. The fire is ignited with stones and carried all across the street. We put cow dung in the fire which frees the air from contamination and harmful germs. During the winter preceding Holi, people usually spend most of their time indoors. Children do not play in the streets. This is the first festival after the winter when children come out of their houses and play games in the streets. The fire kills germs and makes the outdoors safe for children.

We should also note that the Holi fire is maintained daily for a week, and people come on affixed time to sit around and enjoy the heat. This is a centuries-old tradition. In old days, there were no separate playgrounds, and the streets were the only ground for playing. So a child always associated streets with play. In those days, fire was the only way to cleanse the environment and mitigate contaminations.

IV. Past,
Present & Future

Ancient Knowledge

73. What is the contribution of ancient Indians to the modern sciences?

To understand a religion, we have to separate knowledge from the religion. I personally feel that religion is a way of life, and knowledge the core of our strength. Religion is derived from knowledge. Religion teaches us discipline to attain and lead a quality life. Knowledge may be hard to find among the people across the society, but religion is supposed to be followed by all.

Religion is based on the knowledge acquired by scholars and shared through rituals and rules to help the common man understand how to lead a quality life. The sun gives light and energy to all without looking at who gains it. The universe runs without a religion, and it is up to people to believe whether the sun or the moon is superior based on one's own comfort and need. (In Islam, more importance is given to moon as this brings relief for them in desert.)

The Vedas and Upanishads have clearly identified planets and stars, and defined their roles and effects in one's life. I strongly believe that the basic science has come from the Vedas and Upanishads. Astronomy, mathematics, geometry, algebra, and chemistry — they all have basis in the knowledge from our past. When the ancient sadhus and sants undertook research, they passed on their knowledge and findings orally to their students. This may be in form of practical, illustrative examples and sutras (formulas). As the time passed the original form of the knowledge got limited to mere examples and illustrations. Over a period the original knowledge got distorted and only the predecessors' knowledge and preaching become the basis.

Our religious books like *Mahabharata, Ramayana,* and *Bhagwad Gita* are dramatic presentations of the knowledge acquired from the Vedas and Upanishads. Rama and Krishna gfollowed their gurus and weaved their teachings into the character of the common man. Later during the formation of larger societies, the religion (transformed from knowledge) was also needed to be redesigned, reconstituted as per the need of the changing time and place.

The term for self-identification was first given by Indian gurus. The word 'name' comes from 'naam' in the Sanskrit language. As time passed, innovation continued and astronomy was introduced in the education. Later zodiac conditions were linked to an individual birth, and accordingly names, guidelines and predictions were introduced. Moon position at the time of birth was the basis of mental strength, and names denoting such were given to the child. The Hindu religion had a practical role to play in people's lives. This is a big subject and if time permits, I will explain it further in future.

These are some of the examples of Vedic knowledge, concepts and science:

Pushpak Vimana: Ram after defeating Ravana, returned to Ayodhya by Pushpak Vimana. This was a flight of fancy for the common man 200 years ago. Today it is a reality of everyone.

Eclipse: The Hindu science has been predicting for thousands of years the time and place of the eclipses. Our astrologers have been warning us not to see the eclipse with bare eyes without protection. The science has now agreed that the eclipse creates dangerous rays which are harmful to the human being.

Yoga: Indians have been doing Yoga asanas for more than 10,000 years. The world has now recognized it as a science, and have adopted it as one of the essential fitness exercises for the common man. e

We are world leaders in many spheres. Yet we have lost our roots, and adopted fashionable foreign culture for short-term benefits. There is a need to reconcile our self and history. First of all, we must know our own culture and past glory in a right manner. Our rich heritage contains everything to help us lead a comfortable and satisfied life in modern world.

74. Is Sanskrit a dead language? Why should you consider learning it?

Sanskrit is not a dead language despite the lack of interest from the majority of the Indian population. eThe flow of knowledge was limited to a class of people in the society because Sanskrit was considered to be the language of the Brahmins for a long time. Its influence was limited to India in the past, which led to the birth and rise of other languages in rest of the world. Sanskrit is now being rediscovered and adopted in USA, Germany, France and most of the European countries today. Unfortunately due to many years of foreign rule, the education system of India is broken. This is the root of our apathy and ignorance. Sanskrit can never die, and will eventual get its recognition during each period of time and century. Every era in the need of knowledge will come to its shore and benefit from it.

Sanskrit is not a difficult language, particularly for Indians. All the regional languages originated from Sanskrit: Hindi, Marathi, Kannad, Malayalam, Telgu, Tamil, Bengali, etc. This way we have an upper hand over rest of the world. This is a language which has inbuilt music in it, so easy to remember. As per Microsoft engineers this is most computer friendly language. Unfortunately we have never recognized it. I strongly feel that one should at least consider learning the Devanagari script. Parents should teach the alphabets to their children when they are still young and curious, and encourage them to explore the knowledge in our Vedas and Upanishads later.

The irony today is that it's fashionable for our children to learn French, German and Spanish languages, while the western children are inclined to learn Sanskrit and Yoga. We must create interest in our own roots. I strongly recommend such an initiative by our government.

More accurately if we want to learn Sanskrit, we must

learn its grammar as accurately taught by Panini. The Sanskrit scholar and Prof. MK Jha have done great work on it recently. This will help us accurately understand the shlokas and meanings of the ancient Rishis' work on science, mathematics, astronomy and almost all the current and future subject which remain a mystery for rest of the world. The westerns scholars have done great work on this but the same is missing in Indian universities.   en

75. Is there a need to overhaul Indian education? Why aren't we taught Hindu philosophy in our school? Can the ancient knowledge help us earn, compete or live a decent life in the age of science and technology?

It is necessary to appreciate our ancient culture and knowledge, and preserve and pass it on through our education system. If we make the necessary changes to the present education system, I think India can become the world guru without using force.

The present education system in India was introduced by English purely for the purpose to create clerks, assistants, technicians and labor for industries. It wasn't designed to gain knowledge. We acquire degrees and certificates to work for industry or administration, and cannot expect more from the current education. In the materialistic world today, the Guru-Shishya tradition is gone. Present gurus are business partners. They are training managers, who teach only what is designed to teach.

If we want India to reach its full potential and restore the glory of its past, we have to introduce the following changes in our current education system:

- Include Sanskrit as one of the compulsory languages right from the first standard. It is a simple language, which can be learnt faster than any other language. This will bring the person near to the ancient knowledge.

- Start introducing parallel syllabus in Vedic Science on Mathematics, Physics, Chemistry, Medical Philosophy, Astronomy, Economics, and Political Science. Include few chapters in the syllabus comparative to rest of the modern theories.

- Government must promote research centers on Vedic Science and publish the outcome for the common man in multiple languages to show the world the power of our knowledge.

- Promote & patent our ancient knowledge. Mars was known as a red planet in Hindu astrology for more than 25,000 years. Only in the last century NASA took the pictures of Mars and declared it as a red planet. Now people think it was discovered by NASA first, and not by Indian astrologers.

The history is full of examples of worldwide expansion of religions by conversion either through violence, service or preaching. During the Islamic rule, a class of people in India were converted to Islam by forcing them to eat cow meat, Halala meat. Today's so-called Hindus never pardoned them and discarded from Hinduism. The 99 percent of the Islamic population in India were basically Hindus. The Hindus should create systematic mechanisms to bring them back in the Hindu fold by choice and not by force. The government in consultation with the religious authorities must make this a social reform provision similar to what Hare Krishna Mission has done internationally.

Ethics & Politics

76. What role does religion play in our lives and society? Is it really necessary?

There are many definitions of 'religion.' Ever other person the world over has his own views about it. For a common man, the words 'religion' and 'regulation' appear related. Religion or Dharma in Sanskrit means 'duty,' and when duty is not being followed, rules are made. Rules come with penalties. A management body is constituted to judge which A-dharma (non-performance of duty) deserves which penalty to teach people a lesson as a deterrent for others in the society.

Let's imagine how it may have dstarted. Think of a situation where there is no religion, no society. Every man wants to control another man. There is constant fight — it's a "might is right" world. One person, let's call him Philosopher, understands what is happening and starts teaching people about the fneed for a peaceful coexistence. People see the need, and start coming to him to sort all kinds of troubles. Those who follow him fgrow in number — the believers become a dominant force, and non-believers a minority. hAt the same time, multiple people are researching their own areas of interest, and when people start adopting and accepting their conclusions, these conclusions dbecome rules and common beliefs, and this is where a religion is born.

People work hard to money for their loved ones. If there is no law, no rule in society, and a person stronger than you can snatch your money and belongings, would it be acceptable to you? The answer is no. s If we want to lead a comfortable, peaceful and safe life we need to form a society with just rules, and we have to follow those rules and do good work for the society and the world.
y
To believe in God, and to lead a safe and good life are two different things.

77. Why do Brahmins interpret Hindu religion?

We grow up seeing Brahmins come to our house, perform pooja, give advice, take some money, give blessings and go away. And people criticize and make jokes about them.

In the early days of our civilization, Hindu society was divided into four classes of people based on their competence and skills, and not unlike one picking specializations in the modern day education system.

Brahmins: In the past, those who were creative and intelligent were given Yagnopavit and asked to join Rishi-Munies in ashrams. For years they would acquire knowledge, sharpen their intelligence and then return to serve and guide the societys. It was their duty to help enrich the cultural and political spheres of the society by upholding moral and religious values. This was the role of the Brahmins.

Kshatriyas: Some people have good physique, strong leadership qualities and management skills. They would go to an institution like Dronacharya's and learn Dhanurvidya for arms and ammunitions. After completing their studies and training, they would come back to serve the society by ensuring its safety, and protecting it from enemies. The rulers and warriors came from this class of people.

Vaisya: People who had inclinations for trade and commerce i.e. Economics (Arthashastra) came under this category. They learnt techniques of managing money and conducting trade and business from their ancestors.

Shudra: Those who couldn't pursue above fields found other ways to serve the society, including maintaining sanitation and general upkeep. This way they could have a livelihood to support their families.

Everyone's role was defined not based on their birth but based on their abilities. However, over a period a time, the thinking behind this classification was corrupted. It become a class division from birth, and from there on disaster ensued.

78. What is the difference between 'namaskar' and 'handshake'?

Apart from the difference in style, they mean basically the same. Both display our pleasure and gratitude while meeting people, and help convey our regards and good wishes.

By shaking hands, you transfer your energy and enthusiasm to the other person. In Namaste, we join our hands together and bring them near our heart to express our feelings by heart and mind to the other person.

Namaste is a better way to pay our respect. When we do namaste, all bumps and crevices of our hands meet. This is a process in which negative and positive energies come together for the time being, creating an opening for a fresh start for any talk or relationship. And we meet and greet each other with an open mind, without past baggage.

Let me share a personal tip: when you are disturbed and angry, close your eyes and sit in the Namaskar Mudra. You'll start to feel better within a minute!

79. Why does untouchability exist in the Hindu society?

This is the most controversial subject in Hindu religion. Understanding the roots of this tradition will help explain it.

A Hindu society was divided into four classes:

1. Brahmins: Intellectuals, thinkers, researchers, scholars, advisors, teachers and guides to the society.
2. Kshatriyas: Armed forces and administrators who provide safety and security to the society.
3. Vaisya: Entrepreneurs, trade and businessmen, etc.
4. Shudra: Service class, mainly dealing with cleaning and managing waste material in the society.

According to the above classification, Shudras carried out the most unclean or infection-prone work in the society, including disposal of carrion and waste. They were more likely to get infected because of the nature of their work, and if they didn't take care to clean themselves, they could be affected by deadly diseases, which could then spread to others. The ideal thing would have been to educate them about cleanliness and hygiene. Unfortunately, the old rulers and elite classes did not bother educating them as it was not a priority for them. Those at the bottom of the social order were left to take care of themselves with their own limited means and knowledge. A shortcut was rather adopted i.e. untouchability.

Today cleanliness and hygiene is of utmost importance. We have invented tools and technologies to recycle and manage waste, and there is no cause to continue the practice of untouchability. We have toilets with flushes and modern tools to treat dead animals and harmful waste. In olden days this wasn't possible. Sadly, the easy way out was untouchability.

80. Was Gandhi opposed to the elimination of caste system?

Mahatma Gandhi's action revealed that he never challenged caste system. For example:

1. Gandhi termed a class of society as Harijan, which was seen as the continuation of the caste division under a new brand or label.
2. The partition of India was the result of our failure to reform or eliminate caste system. The founding father of Pakistan, Mohammad Ali Jinnah, belonged to a Hindu family which was ostracized by their community for adopting an occupation seen as impure or dirty. His grandfather was a Hindu merchant who went into fishing business in Junagad district of Gujarat — this occupation wasn't acceptable for the Thakkar community, which adhered to Vaishnavism and pure vegetarianism. Jina bhai thought since he didn't consume non-vegetarian food himself, over a period the society would allow him and his family to return to the society. Years later, his children had grown up and ready for marriage, but the Thakkar community continued to refuse to take them back into their fold. He was forced to adopt Islam to wed his children. He took the surname 'Jinnah,' which came from his name 'Jina bhai.'
3. Gandhiji strongly opposed untouchability but did not promote elimination of caste system.
4. Untouchability and Hindu caste system should have been eliminated along with independence.

81. Why are there no social reformers like Swami Vivekananda in India today?

Social reformers are a part and product of the society. These days our focus is more on adopting western culture than promoting social reform. The government must encourage and create space for social reformers to work and address the national's problems. Since independence, there is widespread prosperity but the value of person is going down. We can prevent the loss of our sanskars and values through the following measures:

1. The philosophies of Sanatan Dharma need to be introduced and included in the basic education system right at the primary school. This is the foundation of all the Sanskar in the society.
2. We need to redefine India and Indian heroes for students — we should teach about the lives and philosophies of great social reformers only, and not political leaders.
3. Government should control the so-called gurus, who are destroying the values of genuine gurus.
4. Introduction of Vedic teaching in the primary school.
5. In our education system, first make a person of strong character, a real nationalist, and then build the competency.

82. How do we unite different branches and streams of Hindu sects and communities under Sanatan Dharma? Is diversity the source of strength or weakness for Hindu religion?

Our education system has to improve. The primary schooling should shift from examination centered to Sanskar-centered. The need is to create a right nationalist. Once this is achieved the rest will follow automatically. We have to create hunger for excellence in a growing child. All parents must be assured that a good is always good, and the bad is always bad. In today's world the child is confused between good and bad. The system and the society seem contrary to the values of humanity. Manipulation and cunning are seen as smartness or intelligence. These flawed values being adopted by youngsters today is problematic and damaging. We have to help develop the desire for creativity and constructive action. The values and teachings of Sanatan dharma and Vedas will make a fool-proof society where character will build a person, and persons together will make the society and nation proud and strong.

83. How can we achieve peace in Kashmir? What should be India's approach to Pakistan?

The crisis in Kashmir is recent problem. It is part of India but no other Indian can go and settle there. No one can do business there. How can the central and state governments make rules and prevent progress from reaching the people? This has made this part of the country a cessation — the situation has deteriorated further after independence, and there is no hope for the region if the scenario doesn't change.

Religion-based formation of any nation is not good a solution. A few people cannot and shouldn't be able to decide the fate of a region or a nation. First of all, one has to create an approach towards nation building. There has to be a short-term and a long-term plan.

Consider a logical solution to Kashmir:

1. All efforts should be made to ensure that those who migrated from Kashmir during recent conflicts should be allowed to return with their families to their homes and properties. The state government should make this happen under a direct supervision of the central government.
2. No leader or social reformer should be allowed to promote or preach religion-based demand for segregation which goes against the idea of India. All leaders should be asked to speak about the plan for development, prosperity, education and increase in quality life.
3. Poverty is the main issue in Kashmir and not the religion. If other nations can invest in any part of India, why cannot Indians invest in Kashmir? Small and medium entrepreneurs should be given incentive to come to Kashmir and invest to generate employments.
4. Present form of governance will not help find solution to the Kashmir issue. There should be joint governance between the center and the state.

5. There should a special task force for confidence build-
    ing with representation of Central, State and Army.

There is an urgent need to change the current approach to solving the Kashmir crisis. We have failed to find the answer to this issue in the last 70 plus years. We must focus on development of the region. If we have to amend the constitution to deliver peace and prosperity, we must do it. We should have all-party representation to a forum to find quick and permanent solution to such issues above all political interests.

84. Today we have reached the peak of adharma in Ka-lyuga. When will the new avatar of Lord Vishnu come to rescue humanity and usher in an era of truth, justice and freedom? What should be expected of such an avatar?

Avatar will not take birth automatically if there is no demand for it in the society. When 99% of the human population feel the intense desire and need for an avatar after the society collapses, the birth of an avatar will take place. This doesn't seem likely to happen anytime soon.

In the society, following conditions must be met before any avatar come to our rescue:

1. No respect for Dharma.
2. No respect to fundamental rules for co-existence.
3. The ruler will equate to the God.
4. The ruler will challenge the existence of God.
5. The common man will reach the end of tolerance.
6. There will be extreme pollution and incurable diseases due to the degradation of the nature and the environment. We will not be able to provide for the growing humanity.
7. The law will be made to favor limited class of people.
8. The existence laws of the society will be disregarded.
9. The right people will curse them for their rightness.

The Avatar does not come of its own, we will have to demand for it.

85. What is dharma? How do you determine what is right action or thought, and what is not?

Simply put, dharma is duty either as a citizen, relative or friend, personal and professional, and above all as a human being.

In religion, dharma means faith which comes above all, and connects you to God. It is not compulsory in Hindu religion to seek God. It is also not compulsory for all Hindus to follow a particular god. It is left to the choice of an individual, family, group, or society to follow a particular god and make their own path to reach their god. In a way this is the most democratic and flexible religion in the world.

Religion is a set of beliefs based on a body of knowledge and customs that lead to the betterment of humanity, and also a path to reach to God. It is not only necessary to follow Dharma — fulfill one's duty and obligations — but one has to move further to reach God. All dharmas are part of the great Sanatan Dharma. One must first choose a path and then follow it steadfastly.

86. What is Ahimsha? Why are there so many wars and so much mindless violence around the world? Is peace unattainable?

In a way the meaning of Ahimsa is respecting each other and ensuring coexistence in the world.

s T ghe human mind has the ability to retain memory, think and imagine, which makes Homo sapiens uniquely intelligent and creative of all species on Earth. This also makes him desperate to acquire and hoard more and more. In the course of our evolution, the basic needs of our species expanded from food to safety, love, authority, territories, domination, and so on — which shas resulted into a sense of supremacy.

With supremacy came terror (himsa) among individuals and groups. A common set of beliefs was used as a religion to bring together like-minded people to form a group identity. And the open and true exchange of knowledge and ideas was blocked by those in charge or power. The rulers started manipulating and using the religion as tool to make bigger and bigger circles to make sure that they remain powerful for a long time.

In today's polarized and confused environment, there is a need to open up knowledge and education. dThe principles of Sanatan Dharma can play a big role in achieving world peace. The world has witnessed freedom through Ahimsa or non-violence in India and South Africa. Hindus have never attacked any outside territory. The Hindu population has directly or indirectly worked for the development of human societies and we have a lot to deliver to the world.

I believe India and Indian philosophy can play a more significant and influential role in guiding humanity toward a glorious and peaceful future.

87. How can we establish the rule of law and dharma in the world?

We have come a long journey from lawlessness of the jungle to the present world order. A society where the strong protects the weak as a moral obligation is a just one; a society where the powerful bears the responsibility to protect the weak, and people don't steal or cheat as their way of life is a good one . The ancient scholars and Rishi-Munis developed the theory of dharma to make rules for both rulers and the ruled. These measures became the unspoken constitution which helped instill order and discipline to make sure that the society developed and prospered.

People want a comfortable, healthy and fulfilled life for today and tomorrow. The fears of uncertainty lead even the powerful to seek blessings and care under the protection of the God. However, man's insatiable greed has created more confusion, attachment and dependence, excessive materialistic needs and desires. He is always worried and afraid of the future and uncertainty in life.

What is being experienced today by the modern world has already been experienced by Hindus thousands of years before. This is a religion which focuses on exploring, understanding and achieving a purpose of life through laws of Karma; the theories of soul and body, birth and death, desire and moksha. The developed world has attained liberation but not moksha. The world is slowly turning to Hinduism for guidance and answers, and the day is not far when all world religions will find shelter under the Sanatan dharma.

89. How did the Hindus come up with the concept of swaraja — freedom and democracy — and gave it to the world?

India is considered to be the birthplace of democratic values and ideals. The ancient thinkers and philosophers introduced the ideas of swaraj — self-rule or independence —and Ram-Rajya, a state ruled through a democratic system. It was Rama who gave right to every citizen irrespective of his class or caste to challenge the decision of a king nearly 10,000 years ago. In a way we are the oldest democracy in the world. The western democracies don't come closer to attaining the kind of democratic tradition and institution we have had in the past.

The party-based system of governance where we send our so-called representatives to the parliament has been proven to result in a flawed and imperfect democracy. The elected leaders are governed by his party, boss, self-interest, and ambitions, and a large group of people that he represents. There is no mechanism by which he can be questioned or held accountable for his actions, or lack of it. In Rama-Rajya, even a washerman could question Rama, and he had to take appropriate action. Whether their demand was right or wrong is a different discussion. The fact that even a king had to listen to even a not-so-powerful citizen of his state speaks volumes about our democratic heritage and tradition.

The Hindu concept of ahimsa or non-violence became one of the most effective tools for the birth of the largest democracy in the world. Mahatma Gandhi adopted Vedic concepts and tools, including Satyagraha (non-cooperation), in his struggle for India's independence or swaraj, which he defined as the right to self-rule.

India was a self-reliant civilization, and we could be the same once again with the flourishing of Hinduism in its best form through religious, social and educational reforms.

90. How were the Mughals and the British able to conquer India? How can we make sure that this doesn't happen again in future?

The basic difference between Hinduism and other religions in the world is how we see life and death. We believe the soul takes a new body after death, and that the state of our present life is determined by our karma from our previous life or lives. We believe in connecting with the God and leaving materialistic world behind. The Islamic or Christian forces that invaded India were driven by materialism and scarcity, while we have been driven by our spiritual values and needs.

In Hinduism, the Varan Vyavastha divided the whole community into four major castes for the proper functioning of the society. This system was over a period of time codified and used by those in power for their own benefits. While the system was first based on individual competency, it was later converted into a family business, and thus divided the populations into groups and weakened its unity. The classic example is Upnayan Sanskar (Ygnopavit). Had it been the birth right of Brahmin, there wouldn't have been the need for these Sanskar. A child doesn't become a Brahmin by birth — he has to acquire the Sanskar and Vedic knowledge to become a Brahmin.

If we want Hinduism to spread in every corner of the world, we have to learn and adopt the following changes in the national attitude and beliefs:

- The Varna Vyavastha has to shift from birth to one's competency. Dr. Bhimrao Ambedkar was born into a Shudra family. He rose to the level of one of the most prestigious scholars through the society's patronage and hard work. He was the principal architect of India's constitution, which is considered one of the best constitutions in the entire world. We must remember that there was nothing like reservation for SC/ST during the pre-independence era. If he could rally support and accomplish his vision in the closed and conservative era, why not others?

- The universities must focus on the Vedic education and create required courses for students to opt and later have full-length academic and research opportunities for career.

- Hinduism and its values need to be taught in primary classes to form the spiritual roots and character of the child. If such a program is possible in western countries like USA, UK, France, and Germany, it is possible here in India.

- Sanskrit must be made compulsory up to the 10th standard with introduction to the Vedic knowledge.

- Universities should not copy courses and syllabi from western universities, but introduce MBA/management courses based on Chankya's Arthashatra, his economic principles, and political guidelines from Manu Smruti. In my opinion, Manu-Smruti is wrongly interpreted. It provides a perfect social science, and also talks about guidelines for a ruler. It has much more to contribute than the caste and creed management.

- Lastly, we should feel proud to be Hindu. We should not copy the western culture for fashion, but respect our own religion for its merits. The role of government comes later. First we must build the strength within our family and society. We must change what is wrong and broken, and introduce or establish systematic resolutions within our religion to make it logical and meaningful.

I intend to write a full book on the rationalized approach to give rebirth to Hinduism in due course.

91. Why is India considered a developing nation? Why is it critical for us to collaborate with people of different nationalities and faiths to build upon the modern foundations of sciences and knowledge to create a better world?

Change is constant — the world is no longer how it was a thousand years ago. People's priorities, attitudes and lifestyles have changed. I agree that we cannot return to our ancient way of life. We have to align our self and our nation with the rest of the world. The size of states and societies have expanded. Free economy has made nations inter-dependent. Competition has increased by multiple folds. This has created many advantages as well as disadvantages. The need for Hindu philosophy in the society and rest of the world has not fallen down — it has rather increased exponentially. We have much to contribute to the world. We need to combine our culture in the modern time with our ancient democratic value system. The world has become materialistic today, and Sanatan Dharma could provide relief from its cut-throat competition and troubles.

India is a developing country in this materialistic world based on different parameters of the developed countries. These parameters are not perfect. If you are a developed country today, it doesn't guarantee that you'll remain the same tomorrow. The definition will change, or the situation will change, and your status will change accordingly. Arab countries like Iraq, Syria, and Libya were developed at one point of time — they had the money to buy anything from any part of the world. In the last decade, everything they acquired have gone to waste. People have no food, water or safety. This could never happen in Hindu religion. Our religion teaches us to be peaceful and tolerant, and it inspires us to resist fundamentalism and tyranny and practice self-restraint, self-reliance and dharma.

We have to establish the links between modern science and modern society with the ancient Vedic science and social guidance. There should be a systematic research and reform through serious studies of our literary corpus. Manu-Smruti is just one of the most misunderstood or misused texts in Hinduism. Literature on other subjects should also be studied and interpreted for the current time and generation:

- *Yantra Sarvatram* by Rishi Bharadwaj on engineering
- *Vaimanik Shastra* by Rishi Bharadwaj on making of airplanes and missiles
- *Shushrut Samhita* by Shushrut Rishi on surgical science
- *Charak Samhita* by Rishi Charak on treatment of various diseases
- *Arthashastra* by Kautilya Rishi on economics, political and social science, lLaw, taxation, etc.
- *Aryabhatiyam* by Rishi Arya Bhatt on mathematics and astronomy
-
- We have a huge body of literature available on poetry, drama, yoga, and other sciences and almost on any subjects which are of importance to the modern society.

It was once the job of the Brahmins to study and interpret these texts. The times have changed. It is now the responsibility of the government to set up or encourage universities, which receive grants, to focus on the mission to rediscover, study and promote Indian classics, Indian culture and values in the world.

The ancient Rishi-Munis cared about the peace, happiness and well-being of the whole world: *Om, Sarve bhavantu sukhinaḥ. Sarve santu nirāmayāḥ. Sarve bhadrāṇi paśyantu. Mā kashchit duḥkha bhāgbhavet. Oṁ Shāntiḥ, Shāntiḥ.* They were motivated and inspired to find answers to mankind's suffering and use the fruits of their research and knowledge for the service of the society. We should embrace and encourage such an open, positive and benevolent worldview and lifestyle.

92. What do Hindus view suicide? Can Hindu ideas and principles save one from economic distress and depression?

Suicide is the result of mental distress, which is curable and manageable. The right astrologer can predict the existence of this metal weakness right at the time of birth. The strong desire for committing suicide exists in the mind of a particular person. This can be avoided by early diagnosis, exercise and treatment. Suicide is a social crime — the one who commits suicide creates problem for the family and the society which s/he belongs to.

Let me share an anecdote with you. When I was working at Hazira plant for Reliance, skilled workers were in high demand as their contribution to the entire operation was very important. I initiated a system which made seniors employees adopt junior employees from our department. One senior officer was asked to develop five junior staff under him. He was not only responsible for their professional training, but also looking into their personal problems. One day I was approached by one of my senior officers with a very unique case. There was a person in his group whose parents had committed suicide. The young man didn't go to his house, and slept outside in the nearby localities.

I called the young man to my office and consoled, guided and provoked him to speak about his plans, desires and dreams, and about setting up a family of his own. It took many months to make him think like a normal man. I met his brothers also. The person took my efforts positively. Months later, my officer came to me one day to report a total collapse of automation. There was urgency to retrieve some important material for exports. However, the material in plant was not retrievable due to the failure of automation. The officer told me that the young man suggested that he could retrieve the material by operating the automation manually. It was a risky operation. I called him in and asked him to explain his entire plan. The plan was convincing. I formulated a techno-operations team and allowed him to operate the system manually. It took 16 hours to retrieve the material. All work was done in most efficient manner and the young man, who was once so depressed, found an opportunity to prove his competency. He was then awarded publicly. He is now leading a respectable and a successful life.

In our life, two things are very important: our heart and our mind. They are contrary to each other and complimentary too. The decision taken has to be logically concluded to one. The ability to use both is available uniquely to each one of us. One has to be trained to use both faculties to counter and evaluate each decision before any action.

93. How can NRI Hindus keep their religion and culture alive outside India?

This is very important and purposeful question. Most of the intellectual and learned people from India are going abroad in search of service, business and improving their quality of life. They go abroad to expand their knowledge and further their studies. Most of them succeed and start loving the place and ultimately settle there. This elevates them personally and materially, and they start enjoying the new lifestyle. After all the materialistic needs are achieved, slowly they start realizing the difference, and start missing the roots. They come to their motherland once or twice a year, and slowly this reduces to once in five or seven years. Slowly this frequency reduces to zero. However, they keep missing their motherland. The Hindus abroad can keep their religion and culture alive by staying true to their roots, values and beliefs — if not all practices.

Space Age

94. What are the threats to Hindu faith? Will it ever decline? How do we save Hinduism from becoming tarnished by radicals and extremists?

The Hindu religion has no threat. It will remain in the hearts and minds of people in every generation, time and period. In a way the current definition of development has become old. Once upon a time English ruled the whole of world, today they have no power of their own. They are dependent on big nations. Russia was a super power; today it is working hard to retain it. Germany, France, and the whole of Europe is struggling to retain their status.

Similarly, the Islamic nations in the Middle East and a part of Europe doesn't inspire much home. They have killed their own people more than others. For a time being, their religions spread across the world. However, in absence of a democratic value system and respect for human life, they are now at war with their own people and each other.

The Sanatan Dharma is more than 25,000 years old. People from all faiths have found shelter and acceptance in India. And they have adopted our ancient values and culture to forge a new community identity which is distinctly Indian. This is the beauty and power of Hinduism — it comes in many forms and with many names. It will not and cannot die for thousands of years to come.

95. What does the future of India look like by the mid- and the end of this century?

Sanatan Dharma will retain its value for a long time to come. It has survived and will survive on its own strengths. However, the future of India is not safe in the present form of system. In the name of democracy the nation has been cheated, and our religion and sacred values have been ignored and maligned for political mileage. We are depriving the coming generations of the ancient knowledge and wisdom, which is a big loss to the nation and the world.

In the past, Sanatan Dharma was a manual for good governance. The religious guidelines were the basis for the formation of rules and laws for individuals and societies. People turn to their religion to learn how they can improve the quality of life and become aware of their purpose in this world. Now most of the countries in the world have adopted the rule of a constitution, and the role of religions have been limited.

It is high time India separated religion from politics. If we are a Dharma Nirpeksha (secular) country as per the constitution, why are political parties discussing religion in the election campaigns and asking for votes in the name of caste and religion? All open discussions on television and public meetings about religion should be limited, if not banned. Insensitive, disrespectful, and politically-motivated religious commentaries and criticisms to provoke violence or division should be punishable by law. The current atmosphere is creating hatred amongst our people. This must be stopped legally, and considered a punishable offense equal to breaking the nation.

The ancient Indian literature should be part of the university education, and there should be government budgets for research and innovation, and the outcomes of these researches should be patented without linking them to the religion. For example, Yoga. How could this be attached to a religion? It is for the well-being of the whole of humanity.

96. What should be India's role in the world? What values or mission do we pursue? How do we use our power of influences and culture?

We must create excellent modern literature based on our ancient literature through universities, awards and fellowships. We must largely patent our researches. We must create management tools based on these age-old principles. We must bring all the existing religion of the world under Sanatan Dharma. Hindu religion is also a part of Sanatan Dharma. The knowledge of the universe and universal sciences have birth to the religion. Under Sanatan which is the basis of all world religions, there could be flourishing of a more vibrant world culture and civilization. Once we are able to achieve this status, there will be peace and harmony in the world. There will be respect for each other. There will be no hatred; there will be love and harmony amongst people, societies and nations.

Sanatan Dharma believes in "Sarva Dharma Sambhav" (all religions are equal) and "Vasudev Kutumbakam" (the whole world is one family). These doctrines must be spread across the world. There should be a department under UN called "Sanatan Dharma Sansthan" to spread religious peace and harmony across the world by bringing together religious scholars from all religion across the world. Let them discuss, participate and make the Sanatan Dharma as the world religion. Under this domain, all religions could have their representation. The aim should be to end the terrorism and promote love and brotherhood to improve overall quality of life. This may be a dream today but we will need such initiatives in times to come. India must take a lead on this project at an international level.

97. As humans prepare to settle on Mars, and become a space-faring civilization, what kind of role do you see for us? What should we do with the challenges and opportunities created by the vastness of the cosmos?

I believe that India and Indian ancient scholars have done a lot since the beginning of time, and much can be achieved by the right application of their knowledge and information contained in all our Shastras. If we use them accurately, we can play the role of a world leader in space industry.

The Indian astrologers accurately calculated time and distances thousands of years before the modern science. The unfortunate part is that we have not done anything after the Vedic times. The world has picked up its pace and has reached to the present level. And it is quite possible that had the present science built upon the knowledge of our past, so much of time wouldn't have had been wasted.

There are many missing links and gaps in our knowledge about the birth and power of atom, nature of stars, black holes and the Aakash Ganga (Cosmic Ocean), the theory of gravity, etc. Much has been said about them in our Vedas and Upanishads. If we can concentrate on this aspect of our knowledge, the world will recognize the power of our Vedic shastras, and India will lead and guide the world towards a new golden age of science.

Conclusion

I have answered the above questions with the best of my knowledge based on childhood lessons from my father and mother. And I hope these explanations would be useful to our present and upcoming generations. The knowledge of Hindu rituals are critical when there is so much ignorance and superstition. Some of these insights would be relevant and others not in today's world. u I believe this book will help in the understanding of the Hindu philosophy from a practical point of view in times to come.

ABOUT

H.V. Bhatt is an award-winning author, speaker and management guru based out of New Jersey, US. With over four decades of leadership experience in large manufacturing, Mr Bhatt continues to provide industry leaders unique strategies on effective management to inspire a culture of excellence and sustainable growth. His awards include a patent for an innovative carton-less packaging which saved 55 lakh trees per annum around the world, including India and America.

To get in touch, please write to hariv.bhatt@gmail.com.

You can find him online:

Website: http://hvbhatt.com.
Twitter: @HVBhatt_Author
Facebook: http://facebook.com/HVBhatt.author

9 788193 766507